£3.50
20/6

SIR THOMAS LAWRENCE

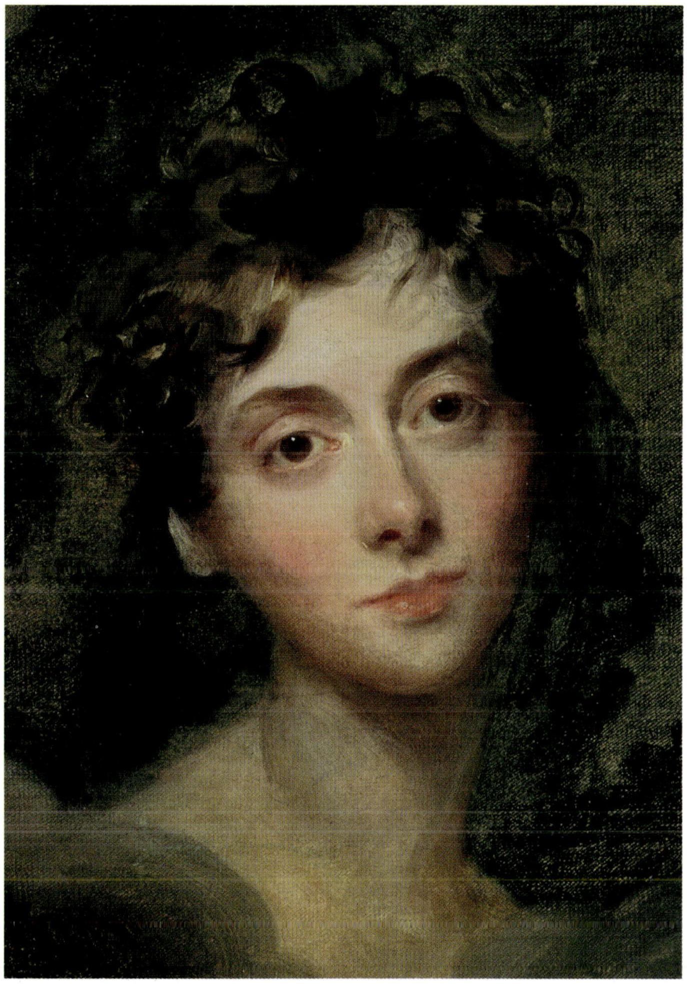

PUBLISHED BY CHAUCER PRESS
20 BLOOMSBURY STREET, LONDON WC1B 3JH

ISBN 1 904449 417

A COPY OF THE CIP DATA IS AVAILABLE FROM THE
BRITISH LIBRARY UPON REQUEST

DESIGNED BY POINTING DESIGN CONSULTANCY

IMAGE ACKNOWLEDGMENTS:
BRIDGEMAN ART LIBRARY
AKG LONDON, SCALA PICTURE LIBRARY
LADY JANE HALLIDAY © ART ARCHIVES – WADDESDON MANOR – EILEEN TWEEDY,
MRS MUSTERS AS HEBE, THE IVEAGH BEQUEST, KENWOOD © ENGLISH HERITAGE PHOTO LIBRARY
FIELD MARSHAL GEBHARDT VON BLÜCHER, COUNT CAPO D'ISTRIA, CAROLINE, PRINCESS OF WALES AND PRINCESS CHARLOTTE, FREDERICK
WILLIAM III, KING OF PRUSSIA, COUNT PLATOV, PRINCE METTERNICH, ARTHUR WELLESLEY, FIRST DUKE OF WELLINGTON, ALEXANDER I,
EMPEROR OF RUSSIA, ERCOLE, CARDINAL CONSALVI, POPE PIUS VII, PRINCE GEORGE OF CUMBERLAND,
THE ROYAL COLLECTION © 2005, HER MAJESTY QUEEN ELIZABETH II
TWO FALLEN ANGELS - PHOTOGRAPH: PHOTOGRAPHIC SURVEY, COURTAULD INSTITUTE OF ART
HENRY BROUGHAM, GEORGE CANNING, ROBERT STEWART,
WILLIAM HENRY WEST BETTY BY JOHN OPIE © THE NATIONAL PORTRAIT GALLERY, LONDON
PORTRAIT OF ARTHUR ATHERLEY AS AN ETONIAN, © LOS ANGELES COUNTY MUSEUM OF ART, WILLIAM RANDOLPH HEARST COLLECTION
THE CALMADY CHILDREN IMAGE: © FRANCIS G. MAYER/CORBIS, ROSAMUND CROKER © CORBIS, ELIZABETH FARREN © CORBIS,
KEMBLE AS HAMLET © CORBIS, HOMER RECITING HIS POEMS © JOHN WEBB/ TATE GALLERY
GEORGE III © HERBERT ART GALLERY, COVENTRY
SATAN SUMMONING HIS LEGIONS © ROYAL ACADEMY OF FINE ARTS

GENERAL EDITOR CHRISTOPHER WRIGHT

TYPESET BY ROWLAND TYPESETTING

PICTURE RESEARCH: VENETA BULLEN AND EMMANUELLE PERI

PRINTED IN CHINA BY SUN FUNG OFFSET BINDING CO. LTD

HALF TITLE; DETAIL OF LADY CAROLINE LAMB

SIR THOMAS LAWRENCE

GEOFFREY ASHTON

CHAUCER PRESS
LONDON

Editor's Note

Geoffrey Ashton's text, written in 1979, is a testament to the enduring legacy of Sir Thomas Lawrence, and the esteem in which he is held. While art historical approaches have changed significantly since the text was written, the author's love of Lawrence's work is apparent in both his style and approach. For this reason I have chosen to retain where possible the author's original words. Idiosyncratic spellings within original correspondence have also been retained.

Susan Lawson

SIR THOMAS LAWRENCE

SIR THOMAS LAWRENCE was one of the three great English portrait painters, along with Thomas Gainsborough and Sir Joshua Reynolds. Like Gainsborough, Lawrence captured the character and fleeting expressions of his sitters' faces with what seems like uncanny accuracy. Like Reynolds, he was able to portray the private person behind the public figure in an endlessly various array of magniloquent poses and gestures. Perhaps more than Gainsborough or Reynolds, Lawrence was able to encapsulate in his portraits the period in which he lived. If the period 1790 to 1830 in English history seems remarkable for the style, elegance, panache and beauty of its key figures, it is largely because Lawrence made them so in his portraits. Lawrence's iridescent images of Romantic sensibility usually met his sitters' requirements of a glamorised reproduction of their outward form and a polite discussion of their inner qualities. Here, I will attempt to ascertain whether or not they also satisfied Lawrence's own intentions and aspirations.

On 5 March 1816 Lawrence was called in front of the Committee of the House of Commons appointed to examine into the qualities and value of the Elgin Marbles. The Committee had to report upon the expediency of purchasing them as a nucleus of a National Gallery of Sculpture and Lawrence was asked by Henry Bankes, the chairman of the Committee, if he thought the marbles were of high enough quality to form a national school of art. Lawrence said that they were and that they would be of essential importance in forming a school of history painting, 'a line of art', he said, 'which I have seldom practised, but which it is still my wish to do'. Though Lawrence never actually used the Elgin Marbles as direct inspiration for his own work, he did plan a large painting of the building of the Parthenon.

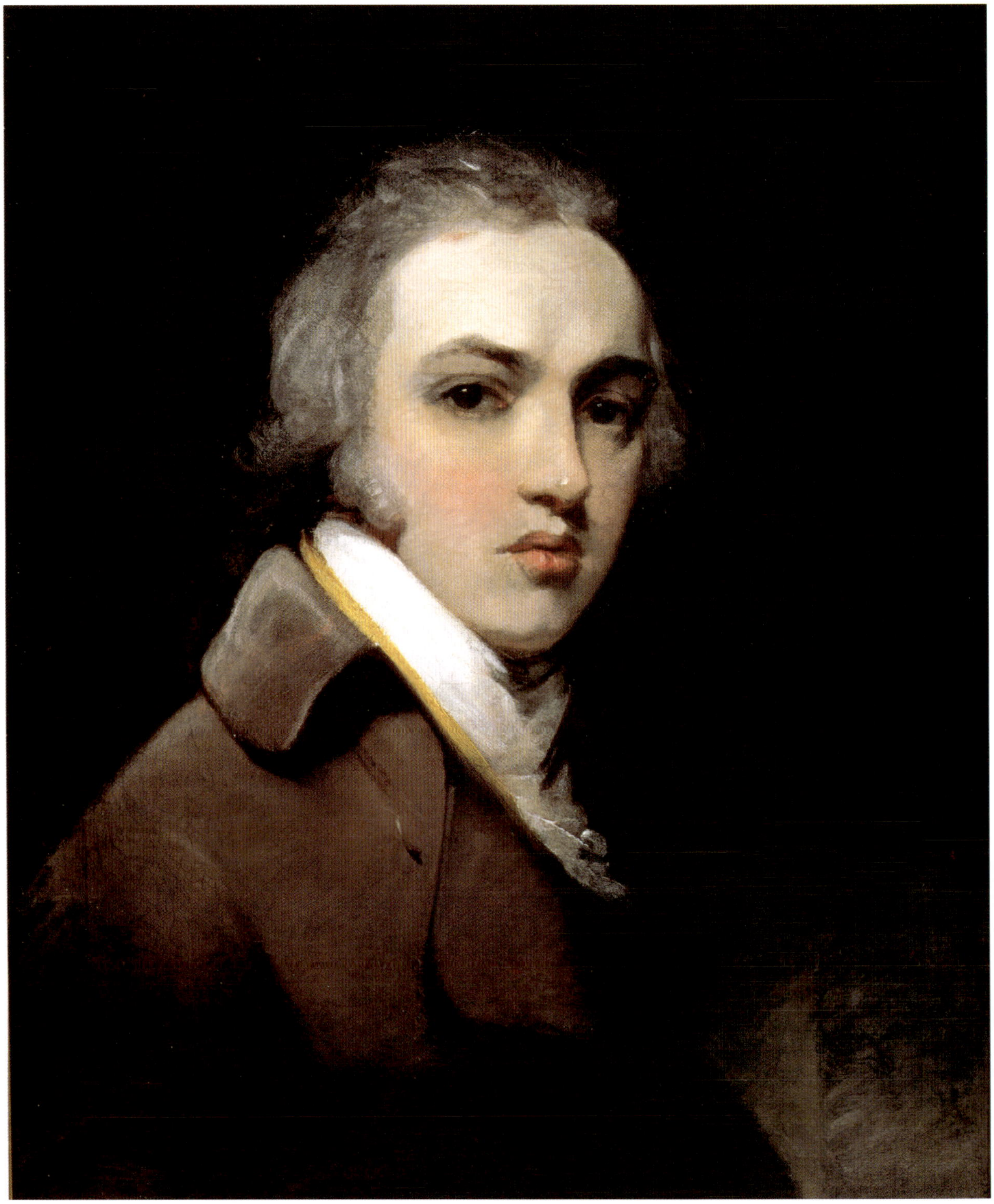

On the other hand, as early as 1787, when he was only eighteen years old, Lawrence wrote to his friend Mary Hartley about, '....the great end of painting, – the expressing with truth the human heart in the traits of the countenance' and in 1821, in his first Address to the Royal Academy students given on the occasion of the annual prize-giving for, amongst others, the best historical work, Lawrence said, 'Composition, colour, arrangement of light and shade, all are lost in the power of expression. It is this, and this alone, that entitles our work to hang in the galleries of monarchs, and by the side of the great efforts of the genius of different ages'.

The potential conflict between Lawrence's wish to be an history painter and his firm belief in the importance of the expressive countenance is the key to his work as an artist. Lawrence followed both his wish and his belief and came up with a solution in his great series of portraits in the Waterloo Chamber at Windsor Castle which, as a group, form not only the climax of Lawrence's career but also the most considerable achievement of British portraiture.

However, the ideal of an image aspiring to the historically sublime tempered by 'the expressing with truth the human heart in the traits of the countenance' meant that Lawrence's attitude to historical sublimity was perhaps rather less rigorous than that of his contemporaries – including Reynolds, Opie and Northcote – working on the Boydell Shakespeare pictures (a lavishly illustrated Shakespeare edition commissioned by Boydell), or than the dictates of Reynolds' *Discourses*. In an undated letter to his friend Mrs Jens Wolff, Lawrence rhapsodised about his picture of the building of the Parthenon, which was never commenced, let alone completed. The heroic forms of the workmen were to be contrasted with

Self Portrait as a Young Man
(oil on canvas)
Victoria Art Gallery, Bath and North East Somerset Council
59½ x 50½ in.

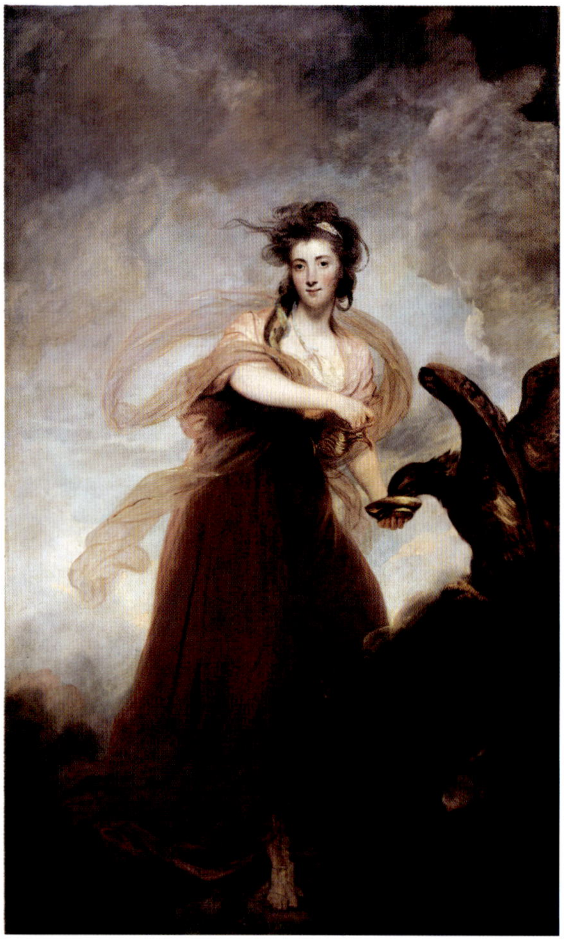

Fig 1
Allegorical portrait, Mrs Musters as Hebe
Joshua Reynolds 1782
The Iveagh Bequest, Kenwood House, London

the 'solemn magnificence' of the group of well-known Athenians below. The most prominent was to be Alcibiades and Lawrence described him in the letter, 'I think that we must give Alcibiades his flowing hair, his indolent graceful manner, and the long trailing of his purple robe'. One suspects that the portrait of *Arthur Atherley* (Plate 6) with his flowing hair and 'indolent graceful manner' would have satisfied Lawrence's image of Alcibiades and the beautiful drawing of *Two Fallen Angels* (Plate 12) shows how soft and sensuous was Lawrence's view of historical sublimity and solemn magnificence.

Nevertheless, Lawrence was one of the most forceful, innovative and original painters of the English school and, with his breathtaking technique, he pulled English portraiture out of the eighteenth century and thrust it into the nineteenth.

In Lawrence's portrait of Sarah Gooden Barret Moulton, known to her family and the world as *Pinkie* (Plate 9), the figure strides or rather leaps into the nineteenth century. Her direct, rather aggressive stare is almost hypnotic and the sense of urgency is heightened by the ribbons of her dress and hat blowing to the left as she glides to the right. A towering banshee-like figure against an equally towering sky, the sense of movement is accentuated by the cork-screw motion of her arms and the clouds behind her.

The crisp directness of *Pinkie* contrasts strongly with the somewhat lurching quality of Reynolds' allegorical portrait, *Mrs Musters as Hebe* (Fig. 1), a woman similarly accosted by the elements. *Pinkie*'s violently expressive sky and broad open landscape are replaced by the fluffy clouds of Olympus. Mrs Musters' clothes are somewhat indeterminate although the otherwise useless gauze wrap is strongly indicative of movement. She feeds ambrosia to Jove's eagle in an alarmingly tilted dish. It is a fine yet, in my opinion, faintly ridiculous painting; the 'floosy' housewife does not appear to know what she is doing in such unlikely surroundings, despite the fact that Reynolds probably had very good reasons for putting her there. She stands on her clouds rather more firmly than Pinkie stands on her grassy slope but she lacks the ultimate directness of Lawrence's portrait, where there is no need for a suggestive or witty allegory. The low horizon, the monumental sky, the incessant movement, the dark-eyed gaze, all combine to present the strongest possible image of a personality. It is perhaps unfair to compare the full panoply of Reynolds' Grand Style with *Pinkie*, a portrait that was commissioned to be painted in 'an easy careless attitude'. In fact, Lawrence is as close to Reynolds in some ways as he is distant from him in others. Reynolds' *Lady Jane Halliday* (Fig. 2) bounds over the landscape in front of a low horizon and similarly towering sky, her hair and clothes blown this way and that by the wind. All these features are used by Lawrence in his portrait, but, unlike *Pinkie*, *Lady Jane Halliday* remains one of Reynolds' team of recently alighted goddesses.

Gainsborough's *Mary, Countess Howe* (Fig. 3), painted with much the same colour scheme as *Pinkie*, is just as direct as Lawrence's picture and perhaps rather more incisive. But what Gainsborough does with a well-behaved flick of the skirt and twist of the toe, Lawrence does with dazzling pyrotechnics, so that the personality of the sitter is almost thrown out of the canvas.

The ability to present a personality in a forceful way seems to have been acquired by Lawrence at some obscure period in his early youth. Certainly, by the time he exhibited his portraits of *Queen Charlotte* (Plate 4) and *Elizabeth Farren* (Plate 5) at the Royal Academy in 1790, he was master of a style that he would continue to follow with minor variations for the next forty years. Lawrence painted these two pictures at the age of twenty, as part of his fourth contribution to a Royal Academy exhibition. *Elizabeth Farren*, at least, caused a stir and, hanging next to Reynolds' rather 'custardy' portrait of *Mrs Elizabeth Billington as St. Cecilia* (Fig 4), provoked the President of the Royal Academy's remark to Lawrence, 'In you sir, the world will expect to see accomplished what I have failed to achieve'. A fact only slightly less remarkable than the pictures themselves was that a twenty-year-old had been commissioned at all to paint the Queen and the most popular comedienne of the British stage.

Fig 2
Lady Jane Halliday
Sir Joshua Reynolds
Waddesdon Manor, Buckinghamshire,
Rothschild Collection

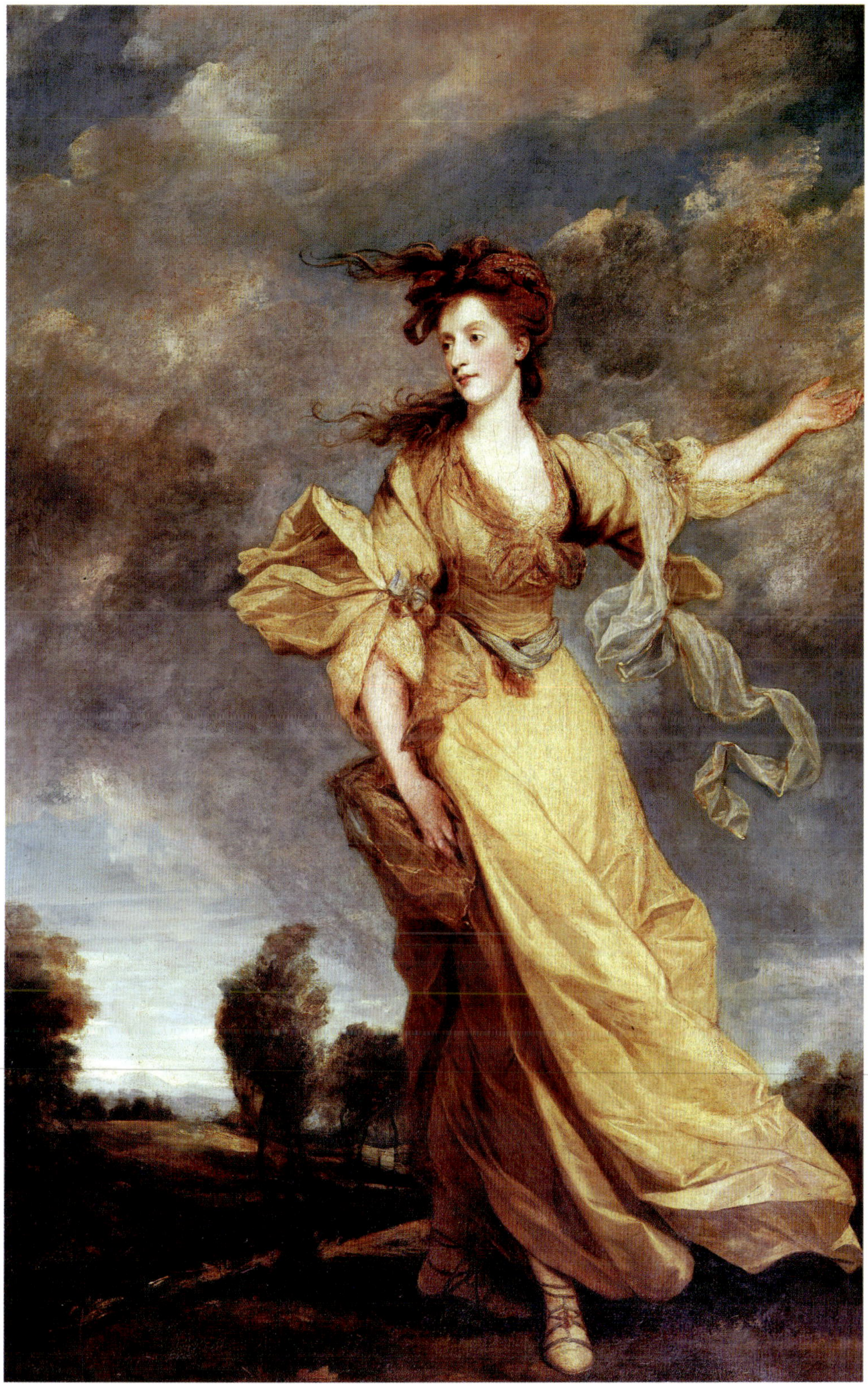

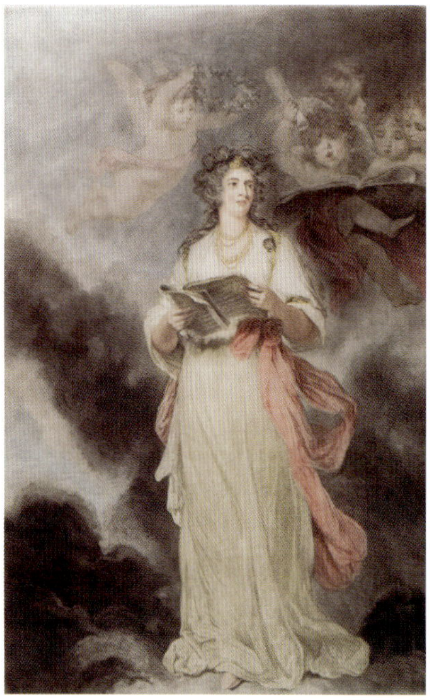

Fig 3 **Mary, Countess Howe** (right)
Thomas Gainsborough *c.*1763-4
The Iveagh Bequest, Kenwood House, London

Fig 4
Mrs Elizabeth Billington as St. Cecilia
engraved by James Ward (1769-1859)
after painting by Joshua Reynolds
1803

From about the age of five, Lawrence had occupied a rather anomalous social position. His father was a failed inspector of Excise in Bristol, a position he left in 1769, the year of Thomas Lawrence's birth, to become landlord of 'The White Lion' in Bristol. In 1773 he moved to 'The Black Bear' at Devizes, a smart coaching inn on the London-Bath road where the infant Thomas was admired for his extreme beauty as well as his ability to draw pencil and chalk likenesses and to recite long quotations from Milton and Shakespeare. The great and famous poured through 'The Black Bear' and there are many stories of Fanny Burney, David Garrick, the Thrales, Mrs Siddons and other notables bouncing the young Lawrence on their knees whilst he spouted or quickly sketched their profiles. In 1779 Lawrence's father went bankrupt for the third time and he harnessed his family's fortune onto the talent of his youngest son, who was now ten years old.

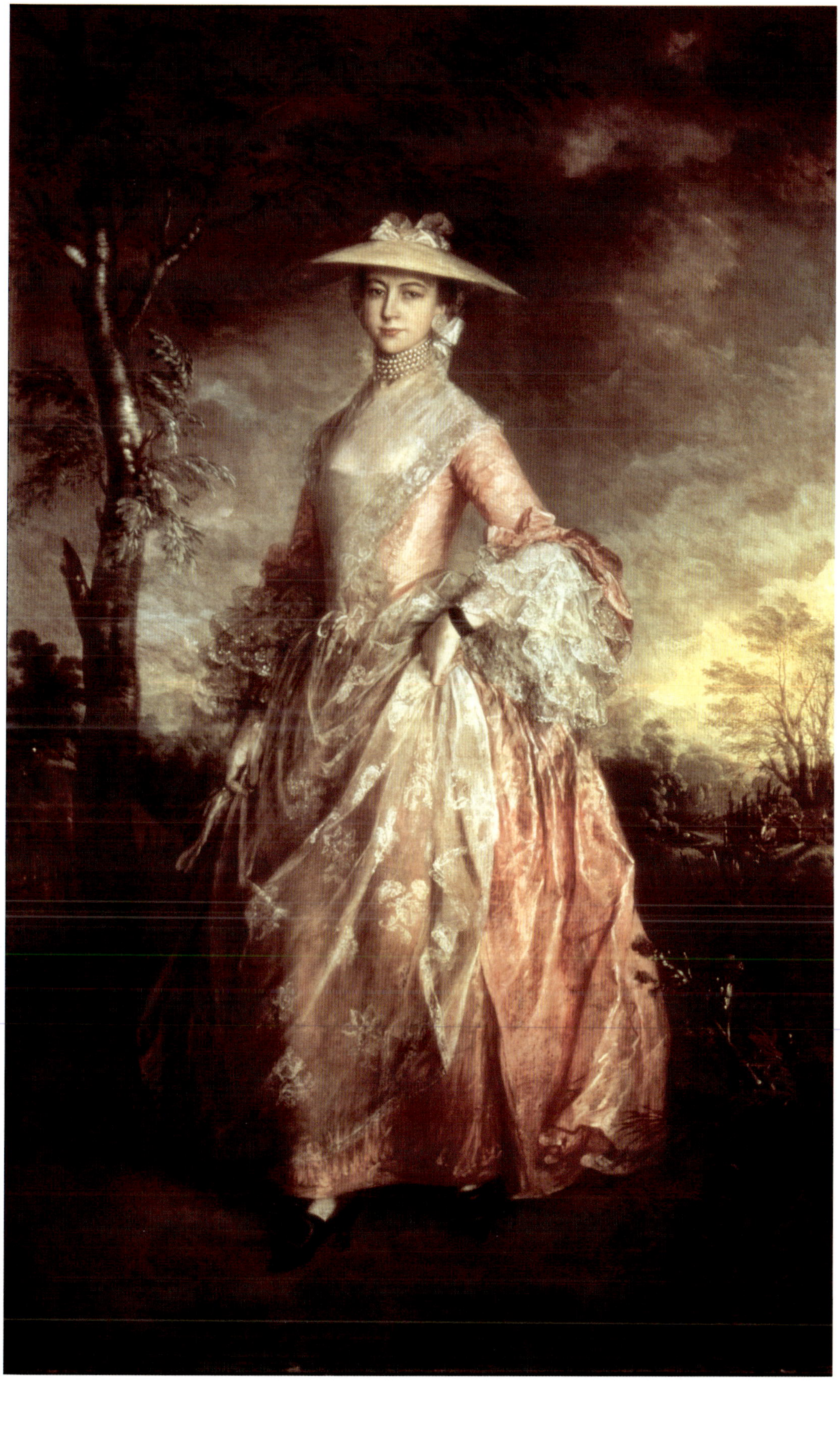

They went to Oxford. The Dons were dazzled by the little boy and subscribed to a portrait of him painted by Prince Hoare, whose father, William, asked if he could send the boy to Italy at his own expense. The proposal was an economic impossibility from Mr Lawrence's point of view and instead the family moved to Bath where a strong eighteenth century tradition in fashionable pastel portraiture existed. The young Lawrence's artistic education seems to have been confined to a few lessons from William Hoare and close studies of the old masters in the surrounding country houses and the town houses of Bath. D.E. Williams, Lawrence's first biographer, tells of an early visit to Corsham Court where the School of Rubens' *Wolf and Fox Hunt* (Fig. 5) was the object of deep admiration. Lawrence would have known the Van Dykes at Wilton but the West Country was not overflowing with galleries of old masters and he would have had to rely mostly on the second-hand inspiration of engravings and copies. In 1785 Lawrence won a silver gilt palette from the Society of Arts for a copy of Raphael's *Transfiguration*. He moved to London in 1787, his family moved soon after and, with the influence of his fashionable contacts in Bath, he was able to build up a clientele. Reynolds helped him to transfer from pastel to oil and he attended the Royal Academy schools for a brief three months at the end of the year. Lady Cremorne, whose portrait Lawrence exhibited at the Royal Academy in 1789 (100), apparently his first full length, suggested his name to the Queen.

Lawrence was summoned to Windsor in 1789 and instructed to bring his 'painting apparatus' with him. He was also to bring some of his pictures 'in crayons and in oil' so that the Queen could see what she was letting herself in for. She seems to have been uncharacteristically bad-tempered whilst she sat for Lawrence. She refused to talk when Lawrence asked her to – he wanted to see her features

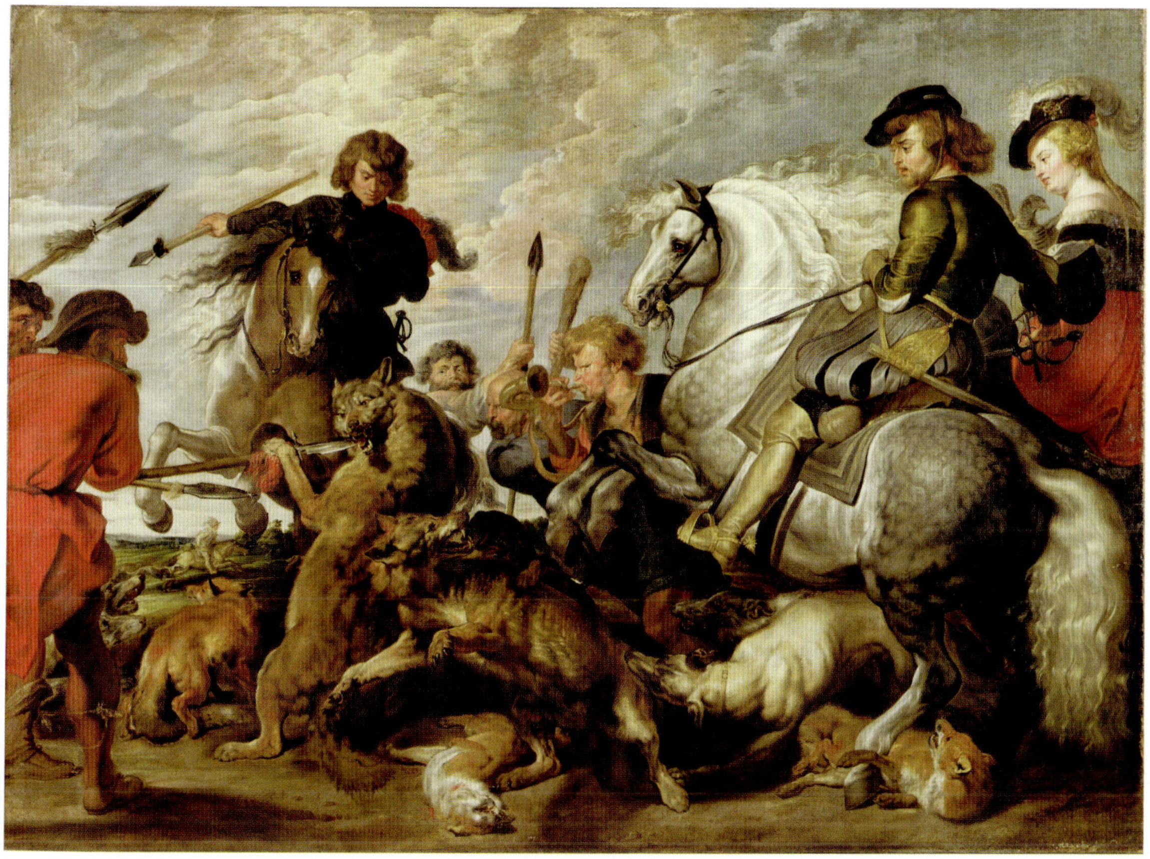

Fig 5

Wolf and Fox Hunt (School of Rubens)

Corsham Court, Wiltshire. Methuen Collection.

animated – and she refused to give him more than one sitting. She did, however, agree not to wear anything on her head, an omission that George III found vulgar and disgraceful. The first impression of the portrait is one of startling informality, a dreamy elderly lady sitting upright in a rather uncomfortable looking chair within a cosy interior, with a view of Eton College Chapel to the left. In fact, there are many indications in this portrait of Queen Charlotte's high position, as well as of her ordinariness. The painting is conceived as a small stage setting; the Queen is raised on a dais like a stage, essentially separated from us, the rest of humanity. A portion of her gown tumbles over the step as a sign of her benign condescension. The curtains and tassels at the top of the painting also frame the stage and the Queen sits in front of a stage flat, the sort that in the eighteenth century was quickly moved on and off stage in grooves. Already the flat has been pulled a little and we see a part of Eton College, itself an example of Royal munificence. When the rest of the flat is removed the Queen will be seated in front of her realms, her head and shoulders carefully placed above the horizon. Her hair is an aureole of glistening grey and the diagonal of shadow that cuts across the picture from top left to bottom right 'magically' jumps over her head. Her intimate connection with the King is shown by his portrait on her pearl bracelet, an identity tag rather than the manacles that have been suggested elsewhere. The fragile old lady is made more fragile still by the peculiar enveloping quality of the chair-back and her short-sightedness can be surmised from the eye-glass hanging at her breast. The shimmering grey-blue of her gown is tempered very slightly by the black lace around her shoulders. Lawrence may have described the Queen as 'an old grey parrot' but this is one of the most touching and sensitive of regal portraits.

The sparkling tintinnabulation of bright paint is seen to even better effect in Lawrence's other masterpiece of the 1790 Royal Academy, the portrait of *Elizabeth Farren*. It was described in the catalogue, much to Miss Farren's mortification, as *Portrait of an Actress*. She felt that *Portrait of a Lady* or *Portrait of a Celebrated Actress* would have been more suitable. There is a much greater sense of freedom in this picture than in the comparatively formal portrait of the Queen. There are no horizontals or verticals apart from the slightly tipping line of the horizon. We are invited into the picture by the hem of Miss Farren's dress touching the bottom of the canvas. She bends slightly to the left and, like Pinkie, seems to be in the throes of a tornado-like spiral movement, towering above the landscape. The wickedly mischievous come-hither look is amplified by it being cast over her shoulder in an off-hand manner and by the suggestion that she is about to turn around and run off to join the sheep in the distance. There might be a reference to a particular prologue or epilogue which Elizabeth Farren was famous for delivering. If so, the reference was, unfortunately, missed by contemporary comment, which took great exception to the Winter garb worn in a Spring landscape. In any event, Lawrence created an especially windy sky to blow Miss Farren's hair about wildly, perhaps to indicate that she was a 'wild, wild' lady. The tousled hair, which was very fashionable for a short period, is reflected by the furry muff hanging at her side and both hair and muff are painted with the same ecstatic but clearly defined strokes. In fact, the head is so overpowering that without the muff to balance it, the picture would be extremely top-heavy. Apart from its compositional value, the dangling muff with its blue ribbon is perhaps a reference to the blue-blooded Earl of Derby who was apparently dumpy and squat – almost the same shape as the muff – and who Elizabeth Farren 'dangled' for many years before marrying in 1797. The Earl of Derby bought the picture after arguing about the price for some time, but Miss Farren was unhappy about it. She wrote to Lawrence in 1792 expressing her dismay, with suitable charm: 'Mr Lawrence, you will think me the most troublesome of all human beings, but indeed it is not my own fault; they tease me to death about this picture; and insist upon my writing to you. One says that it is so thin in the figure, that you might blow it away – another that it looks broke off in the middle; in short you must make it a little *fatter*, at all events, diminish the bend you are so attached to, even if it makes the picture look ill; for the owner is quite distressed about it at present. I am shocked to tease you, and dare say you wish me and the portrait in the fire – but as it was impossible to appease the cries of my friends, I must beg you to excuse me'.

Needless to say, Lawrence did not change the picture and we can still see Miss Farren's unrelenting glance back at the eighteenth century balancing itself somehow on her twisting snake-like body. The

Queen was even more dissatisfied with her portrait and never took delivery of it.

I have considered these two portraits in some detail, since Lawrence's portrait style essentially remained the same for the rest of his life. In a career of many concomitant masterpieces, *Queen Charlotte* and *Elizabeth Farren* are the first two. Lawrence's method is to choose a trait or traits of the sitter's personality, the regal as well as the homely Queen Charlotte; the lively and coquettish Miss Farren. The composition lines or lines of movement combine to express these characteristics and, through the use of a device, the attention is concentrated on the head; by the interruption of the shadow in *Queen Charlotte*, and the dual motif of the muff and the shaggy head of hair in *Elizabeth Farren*. It may seem platitudinous to say that Lawrence concentrated the main effort of his portraits in the faces of his sitters, but this is precisely what Reynolds and Gainsborough sometimes did not do. With Lawrence, the specific replaces the general and all the elements combine to particular effect.

Although many aspects of Lawrence's style remained the same over a long period, a number of things did change, including his use of brilliant white underpaint. This technique was used effectively by the Pre-Raphaelites in order to accentuate the brilliance of the upper layers of colour but Lawrence's method differed from theirs in that the underlying layers of paint were covered whilst still wet and swept into the subsequent layers of paint. This gives a waxy effect that is almost blinding in the case of *Queen Charlotte* and *Elizabeth Farren* when displayed under modern gallery lighting. Later in the 1790s this rather glutinous method became somewhat unpleasant and sticky in appearance and remained so on the rare occasions when it was used in later pictures, such as *Miss Murray* (Plate 47).

Lawrence's paint was generally applied more sparingly as he got older. The profile bust of *George IV* of about 1814 shows the head sloshed onto the prepared canvas with virtuoso freedom and speed.

Lawrence's posthumous sales included a number of quick chalk portrait drawings on these prepared canvases. His usual method was to sketch not only the head but the whole pose of the sitter. He then painted the head whilst the sitter was in front of him; an aura is often visible showing the extent of this initial painting. The rest of the picture would be filled in at a later date, by Lawrence himself or by his studio but following the original composition sketched by Lawrence.

The Lawrence papers in the Royal Academy include a number of letters to and from various correspondents which reveal Lawrence's interest in the technical and chemical problems of oil paint. He owned several canvases illustrating Reynolds' theories of colour composition but he was anxious, no doubt, that his pictures retained the colours with which they were painted; a number of Reynolds' paintings were already fading to pale blue and violet at the end of the eighteenth century. The following extract is from a letter to Lawrence from Charles Macintosh, dated Glasgow 30 March 1810: 'Since my return to Scotland, I very often reproach myself for not having sooner sent you my discoveries upon permanent colours, for painting; perhaps they are not intitled to a better name, and very possibly you have considered the delay as merciful; nevertheless, as I said to you…I am inclined to think the modern discoveries in chemistry have been of no use whatever to the art of painting; on the contrary, that they have been really hurtful to it – a vast superfluity of pigments have been of late years invented; which altho beautiful in themselves, or when recently prepared; on investigation are found to be compound bodies; very frequently saline substances which when mixed together (to produce particular tints) sooner or later act upon, and decompose each other – Again, it frequently does so happen, that the colouring matter of such is a transient and passing nature, not capable of resisting, for any length of time, the action of light and air. With becoming deference I submit to you the following considerations for the choice of colours.....1st. To employ generally only simple substances; and as often as possible, native bodied, which have been found not to act Chemically upon each other, when permitted; and which experience has proved to resist best, the action of light and air. 2nd. To refuse absolutely the introduction of any colour, however beautiful its shade, or however easily it may flow from the pencil until something of its history and qualities is known. 3rd. Be very jealous of the colours denominated Lakes; it would be ten thousand pities, if any of your pictures were to die before you which will infallibly happen if you deal deep in Lakes; generally speaking, their durability is in inverse ratio of their beauty. 4th. Use as few different colouring bodies as possible; your chances will be greater of knowing something of their nature. 5th. Receive every new, or Quack colour, with a trembling hand......'

Although Lawrence's six Addresses to the Royal Academy students, given from 1823 to 1829, tended to concentrate on the importance of expression, composition and line, the 1828 Address included a mention of colour: 'The English School, is now, I believe, generally admitted to be the first in Europe, for the knowledge of Chiaro-Oscuro, the philosophic arrangement of a whole, and particularly for its excellence in colour'. The remark was prompted by the loan, to the Royal Academy School, of one of Lord Grosvenor's Rubenses. Presumably the ebb and flow of colour in the Corsham Court *Wolf and Fox Hunt* (Fig. 5) had impressed the young Lawrence as much as the ebb and flow of the composition.

The fact that one of his friends, Sir George Beaumont, owned Rubens' greatest landscape, the *Chateau de Steen*, does not seem to have inspired Lawrence to change his attitude to the genre. In his early painting landscape is used as a descriptive adjunct to the portrait; in his later work it is hardly used at all, although a number of the Waterloo Gallery portraits are exceptions to this generalisation. *Queen Charlotte* looks out, or rather would look out if she turned round, onto Eton College Chapel. Not only is this geographically correct but, as has been suggested already, it is a reference to the generosity of a Royal forbear. The chapel reappears in Lawrence's 1792 portrait of *George III* (Plate 7). Perhaps the glittering and hardly perceptible distant towers in the landscape of *Elizabeth Farren* are supposed to represent Knowsley, the home of the Earl of Derby. It hardly matters when one reflects that the spring-like landscape indicates a 'spring-like' personality, beneath a blustery sky which also echoes the sitter's temperament.

Eton College Chapel appears again in the portrait of *Arthur Atherley*. As the picture was exhibited at the 1792 Royal Academy as *Portrait of an Etonian* this is not in itself surprising. However, Lawrence's later Eton leaving portraits do not have explanatory views in the background, nor does the portrait of *Sir Charles Lowther*, painted in the late 1820s. The point to note is that while the pose has remained the same for over thirty years (although here it is in fact reversed), down to the hat held in one bare hand and the spare glove in the other gloved hand, the explanatory landscape has not. There is no indication of Lowther's blindness apart from his seemingly vacant stare into nowhere.

This quality of succinct understatement is also found in one of the finest of Lawrence's late portraits, that of *Henry Brougham, 1st Baron Brougham and Vaux* (Plate 44). The highly intelligent face of one of the ablest men in the government gleams supernaturally against the dark red drapery, which darkens around the head to show off the features more precisely. The gaze is casually directed from the face to the hands which have the same supernatural glow and which rest on a bundle of documents.

At the same time, Lawrence could produce as 'gushing' a painting, that is either overtly attractive or supremely repellent dependent on one's point of view, as his portrait of *Louisa Georgina Augusta Anne Murray* (Plate 47). With the sticky paint, coy expression, peculiar anatomy of the arms, rouged cheeks and lipstick, and laboured iconography (the flowers in her dress refer to the various female saints whose stolen food for the poor turned to flowers when they were caught by their wicked husbands or masters) this picture might lead one to believe that Lawrence had gone decidedly downhill since his consummate masterpieces of 1790.

Yet one can turn quickly to a portrait of the same period such as that of the elderly *William Wilberforce* (Plate 51) whose twinkling yet questioning eyes, his fine features though rather large nose, and his mouth which seems about to form some sentiment of freedom, show Lawrence at his most expressive, economic and intimate.

Lawrence's early dictum of 'expressing with truth the human heart in the traits of the countenance' is manifest in many of his portraits, most sensitively conveyed perhaps in the later works. There is, however, an excited sense of theatre in even the most dignified of these portraits and before tracing Lawrence's development as an history painter up to the Waterloo Gallery pictures, it is useful to recollect his connections with the live theatre. David Garrick is supposed to have asked the young Lawrence whether he would prefer to be a painter or an actor. The boy was an experienced public reader and the stage was a real alternative as a career. In later life he took a lively part in amateur theatricals, especially those of the Marquess of Abercorn at Stanmore Priory in front of the Prince of Wales and Sheridan. Sheridan said that Lawrence was, '*really* a very good actor'. He was intimate with actors throughout his life and regularly went to the theatre. So far as we know, the greatest emotional upheaval of his life was over Mrs Siddons and her two daughters, both of whom he pursued from 1795 and both of whom later died heartbroken, Maria in 1798 and Sally in 1803. He was familiar with theories of theatrical gesture; Mrs Siddons' son Henry's *Practical Illustrations of Rhetorical Gesture and Action, adapted to the English Drama*, 1807, based on the German version of Engel, was one of the most important books in English on the subject in the early years of the nineteenth century. He was also a close friend of John Philip Kemble, Sarah Siddons' brother, who was the intellectual as well as the practical head of the new grand style of acting. Apart from his earliest attempts at the genre, Lawrence's history paintings refer directly to the theatre. They might be read as theatrical portraits but Lawrence saw his grandiose works of around 1800 quite specifically as history pictures.

The theatrical gesture was still very much in evidence in the larger portraits that Lawrence painted in the 1820s, such as the full length painting of *George Canning* (Plate 48). This painting, or a similar version, was criticised for showing empty benches in the House of Commons, something that did not happen when Canning was, 'Calling into being the New World to redress the balance of the Old'. Canning's gesture, one of the many Lawrence inspirations that were copied for Victorian Town Hall Portraits and Town Hall Square Statues, perhaps has an ultimate source in one of the Raphael Cartoons, such as *St. Paul Preaching at Athens*. A more immediate and specifically theatrical source is Opie's splendid portrait of the wonder boy, *Master William Henry West Betty, playing Young Norval in John Home's tragedy Douglas* (Fig. 6). Master Betty was at the height of his short-lived fame when it was shown at the Royal Academy in 1805. An unlikely source, perhaps, for the portrait of a political leader but quite appropriate to Lawrence's way of thinking and perhaps quite apposite for a portrait of a man whose mother had been an actress and who was given to theatrically resplendent political actions and statements.

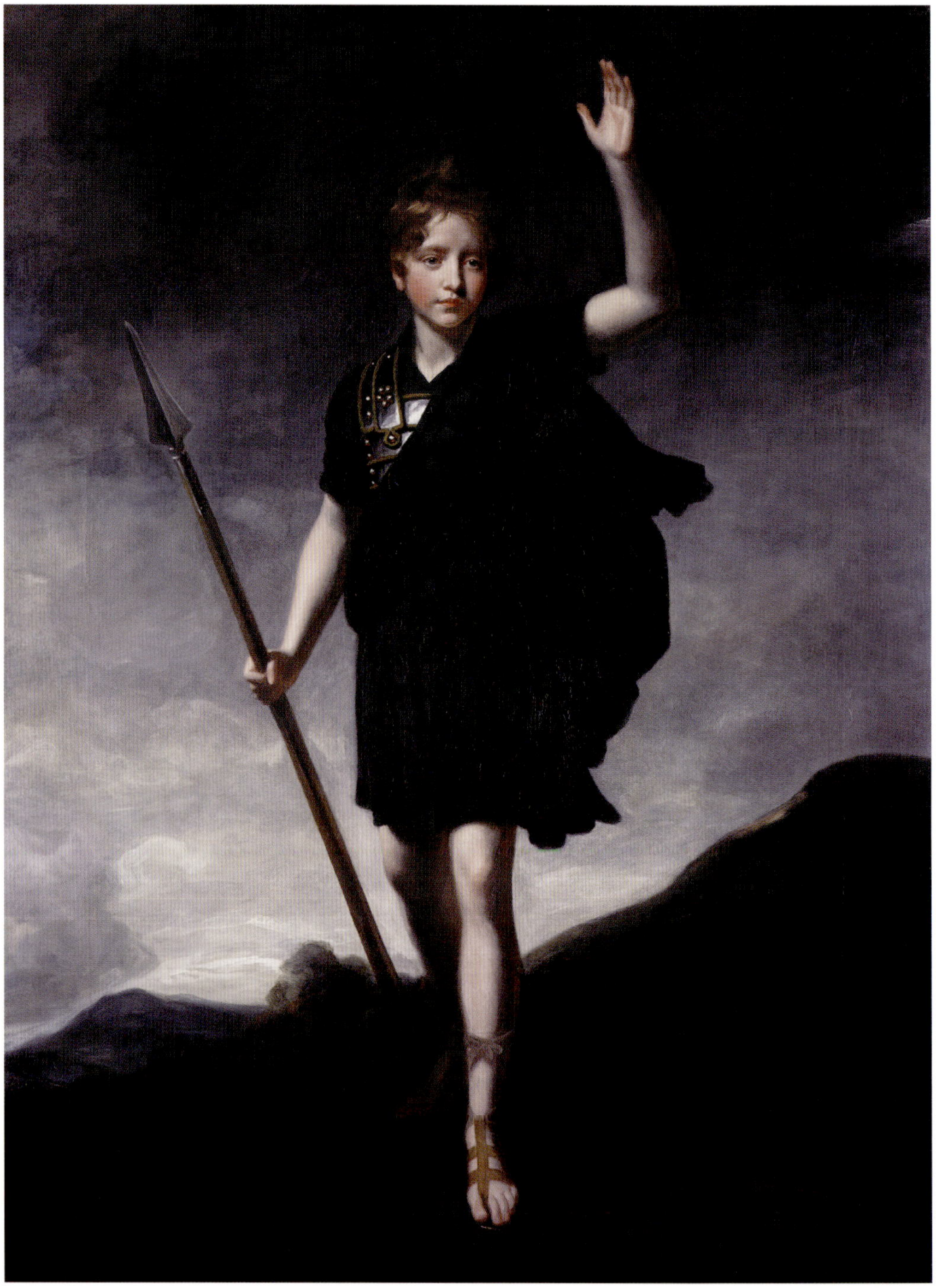

In Lawrence's first history painting to survive, the art-historical references flow thick and fast, Raphael's *School of Athens* and *Parnassus* being much the most important. *Homer Reciting his Poems* (Plate 1) was commissioned by Richard Payne Knight, in 1788 according to Williams, although it was not shown at the Royal Academy until 1791, and is a surprisingly small picture – only 37 x 43 in. It shows an accomplished sense of composition and despite the rather unsuccessful use of thickly applied green paint, one feels the force of a much larger work trying to get out of this crowded and somewhat self-conscious picture. Lawrence's next history picture was five times as large as the *Homer* and the subject was taken from Shakespeare. Although Lawrence painted another picture over the top of his *Prospero Raising the Storm*, and there is no evidence at all as to the appearance of the picture, the subject matter suggests that he was trying to concentrate his historical efforts into the 'expressive countenance' of a single figure. *Prospero* was shown at the Royal Academy in 1793 (191) and, for some reason, there does not seem to have been any critical comment. Lawrence was sufficiently discouraged to wait until 1797 before exhibiting another history piece. In the meantime both Covent Garden and Drury Lane had opened their enormous new theatres designed by Henry Holland. (In fact Covent Garden was opened right at the end of 1792; Drury Lane followed in 1794.) The enormous increase in size of the auditoria changed the theatres from the small intimate places they had been, where there was great rapport between the audience and the actor, to the huge barns where the actor was seen from a considerable distance. The style of acting had to change as well, so that voices became more hysterical and gestures became more emphatic.

Fig 6 **Master William Henry West Betty, playing the young Norval in John Home's tragedy Douglas**
John Opie, 1804
National Portrait Gallery, London

Lawrence was influenced by this broader style of acting in the development of his grander pictures. In the first of these, *Satan Summoning his Legions* (Plate 13), the theatrical influence is perhaps not as evident as in the later pictures. The theatrical flicker of the infernal regions lights up the rather surprising body of Satan, striding across the fiery sea and elongated into a very imposing image. The picture is enormous, over fourteen feet high and nine feet wide, but Lawrence still manages to concentrate the gaze on Satan's burning coal eyes. Lawrence always considered it his best work and it provoked a great deal of comment when it was exhibited. The general bias was in its favour but Pasquin's opinion is remembered because, as usual, his comments were the most witty: 'The picture is a melange made up of the worst parts of the divine Buonarotti and the extravagant Golzius. The figure of Satan is colossal and very ill-drawn; the body is so disproportionate to the extremities, that it appears all legs and arms and might at a distance be taken for a sign of the spread eagle. The colouring has as little analogy to truth as the contour, for it is so ordered that it conveys the idea of a mad German sugar-baker dancing in a conflagration of his own treacle'. Not unnaturally, Fuseli accused Lawrence of copying from him. Lawrence replied that he had modelled the pose on one he had seen Fuseli himself take, high on a cliff top. Lawrence's is perhaps the more disputable statement.

The following year Lawrence achieved a less controversial solution in what is perhaps the finest of his strictly, or mainly, historical pictures: *John Philip Kemble as Coriolanus at the Hearth of Tullus Aufidius* (Plate 15). The already imposing figure of the great tragic actor is blown into heroic proportions. Like Queen Charlotte, he is raised on a step above the rest of mankind. With his foot firmly on the step, however, he makes no attempt to come down from his elevated position. The incident in the background is deliberately murky and the emphasis is on his noble countenance framed by the black curls of his hair, which give the impression of a laurel wreath.

John Philip Kemble as Rolla in 'Pizarro' was painted over *Prospero Raising the Storm*. *Pizarro*, adapted by Sheridan from the German play by Kotzebue, was the most popular tragedy since Home's *Douglas* in 1756 and the picture was one of the most popular images of the early nineteenth century. The Duke of Wellington later wanted to take it to Paris as the centrepiece of the British Embassy. The body was modelled from Jackson, a professional boxer who Lawrence is supposed to have fought and beaten at an early age, but the face is the ever-noble visage of John Philip Kemble, who created the part of the Inca hero at Drury Lane in 1799. In the case of both the *Coriolanus* and the *Rolla* Lawrence has used a current theatrical success as an inspiration for a work of historical pretensions, something his contemporaries were particularly anxious not to do. Romney's allegorical portraits of Lady Hamilton are the nearest equivalent but Romney did not have the inbuilt advantage of Kemble's distinctive profile.

The next historico-theatrical work was *John Philip Kemble as Hamlet* (Plate 20) and the last, after a gap of some years, was *John Philip Kemble as Addison's Cato*. The former was bought, in 1812, by Mr Maddocks M.P. who wanted to use it as the high altarpiece of the church in his newly built Welsh village of Tre Madoc. The Bishop of the Diocese refused to support the idea but it is a reminder that Lawrence was not the only person who regarded his large historical pictures as modern equivalents of the Baroque altarpiece.

'In you sir, the world will expect to see accomplished what I have failed to achieve'. Perhaps Lawrence's heroic portraits of Kemble come closest to what Reynolds expected to see him accomplish. Lawrence always saw himself as the true successor to the First President of the Royal Academy and the beacon of the English School. He succeeded Reynolds as Painter in Ordinary to the King and as painter to the Dilettante Society. (He was painting copies of Reynolds' state portrait of George III as late as 1815 – the King presumably being dissatisfied with Lawrence's 1792 portrait of him.) Lawrence was appointed to both these positions before he was made a full Academician. He attained this particular honour in 1794, before he was twenty-five. Envied by his vastly inferior contemporaries, Lawrence was regarded as something of a whizz-kid in the 1790s and his efforts at history painting were evidently partly inspired by a wish to rise above his reputation as the darling of high society. When he became President of the Royal Academy in 1820, Lawrence took his position as titular head of the British School of Art very seriously indeed. His encouragement of young artists was genuine and useful as well as being self-effacing and whilst his Addresses to the Royal Academy students do not approach Reynolds' *Discourses* in terms of literary quality or pre-digested theory, they contain a wealth of practical advice. Time and again the students are referred to the example of Reynolds.

There was at least one occasion on which Lawrence painted in direct competition with his hero. Reynolds' triple portrait of *Lord Ashburton, Lord Lansdowne and Colonel Barré* was commissioned by Francis Baring in 1787. Lord Ashburton was his brother-in-law and all three were his close political friends. Thirty years later, then a Baronet, he commissioned a pendant from Lawrence. Slightly larger than the Reynolds, it shows Sir Francis Baring himself with his business associates, John Baring and Charles Wall (Plate 23).

Reynolds' picture is a masterpiece of characterisation. Three stolid figures, firm and immovable, represent the ruling class in action, or rather, in this case, inaction. The impassive nature of the poses and the composition is reflected in the resolute expressions. It is a static picture in which Reynolds transfers the momentary into the perpetual by capturing a precise moment, a precise pose.

The Lawrence is a much livelier work although Sir Francis, in black on the left, is given a pose that directly mirrors the Reynolds. As befits a pillar of the community, he is placed in front of a column, a fully rounded piece of architecture rather than the discreet pilasters of the Reynolds. He sits in a splendid, almost papal, chair and is positioned so that the viewer looks down on the two 'lesser' men to the right. They sit at a table which is painted with all the perspectival complexity of a late Cezanne and which is an integral part of the composition rather than an excuse for the pose, the part the table plays in the Reynolds. They are poring over a ledger but start up to look at something to the left, beyond Sir Francis. In fact they are looking straight into the Reynolds which hung next to them. Sir Francis, on the other hand, intuits what the others need to see and, looking away in the opposite direction, reflects on his three old friends, the last of whom, Lord Lansdowne, died in 1805. Reynolds, in the *Eighth Discourse*, says, 'What is done by painting, must be done at one blow'. He captures the pose that expresses the character of his sitter or sitters. Lawrence manages to do this, with wit, and with theatrical flair.

Sir Francis Baring was an immensely influential man, Baring's Bank being one of the chief financial supports of the British Government throughout the Napoleonic Wars. He was also Lawrence's banker and managed to keep him solvent despite the fact that the artist was insanely incapable of organising his own finances. One of the reasons that Lawrence's enormous income from his practice always seemed to melt away was the vast amount he spent on his collection of drawings; probably well over seventy thousand pounds altogether. The collection, which was the finest in existence at his death, was inspired by the example of Reynolds' own collection of old master drawings.

Lawrence also possessed one of the finest of Reynolds' portraits, *Lord Heathfield of Gibraltar* (Fig. 7). He copied the pose of the soldier, petrified into the rock of Gibraltar itself, in his portrait of *Charles, 1st Earl Grey* (Plate 8) and adopted Lord Heathfield's rugged nonchalance in many of his other portraits of soldiers.

Reynolds' studio posing chair, also owned by Lawrence, is allegedly the throne visible in one of the pictures most deeply revered by him, Reynolds' *Sarah Siddons as The Tragic Muse* (Fig. 8). In Lawrence's panegyric on Reynolds in his first Address, this portrait, like that of Lord Heathfield, is singled out for particular praise. He says: 'It is singular, that the judgement, the unpretending sense, and manly simplicity, so generally acknowledged to have marked the character of Sir Joshua, should have been impugned only on those opinions upon Art, which seem to have been most deliberately formed, and were enforced by him with parental zeal, as his last remembrance to this Academy. Sufficient proof of the sincerity of his admiration of Michael Angelo, had previously existed, in the actions of some of his finest groups having been taken from him; but we want no other evidence of its truth, than his picture of Mrs. Siddons; a work of the highest epic character, and indisputably the finest female portrait in the world'. He continues, 'The link that united him to Michael Angelo, was the sense of ideal greatness, the noblest of all perceptions. It is this sublimity of thought, that marks the first rate genius; this impelling fancy – which has no where its defined form, yet everywhere its image; and while pursuing excellence too perfect to be attained, creates new beauty that cannot be surpassed'.

Lawrence's own 'sublimity of thought' is everywhere abundant in his large historical pictures. His particular ability to link this with 'expressing with truth the human heart in the traits of the

Fig 7 **Lord Heathfield of Gibraltar**
Sir Joshua Reynolds, 1787
National Gallery, London

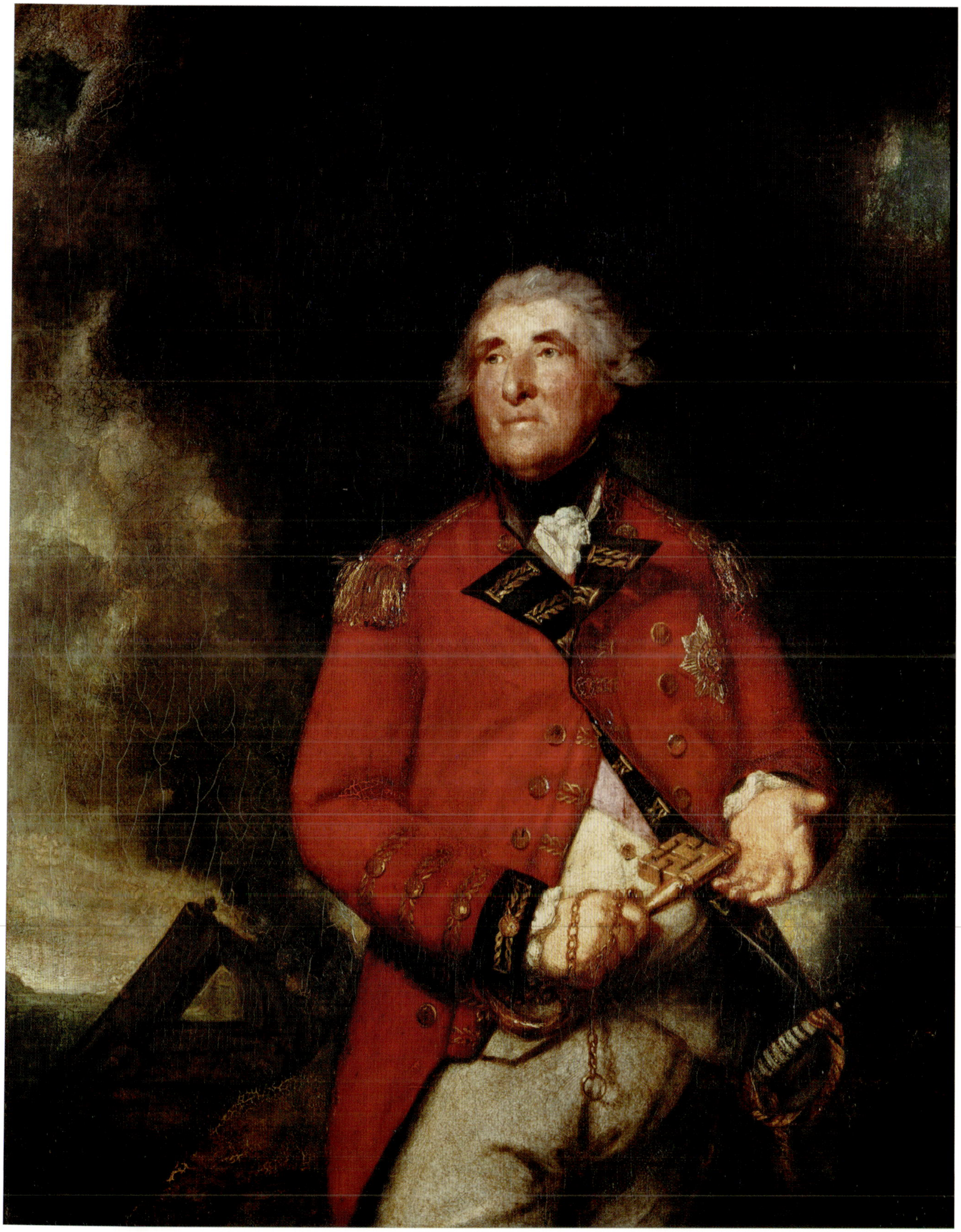

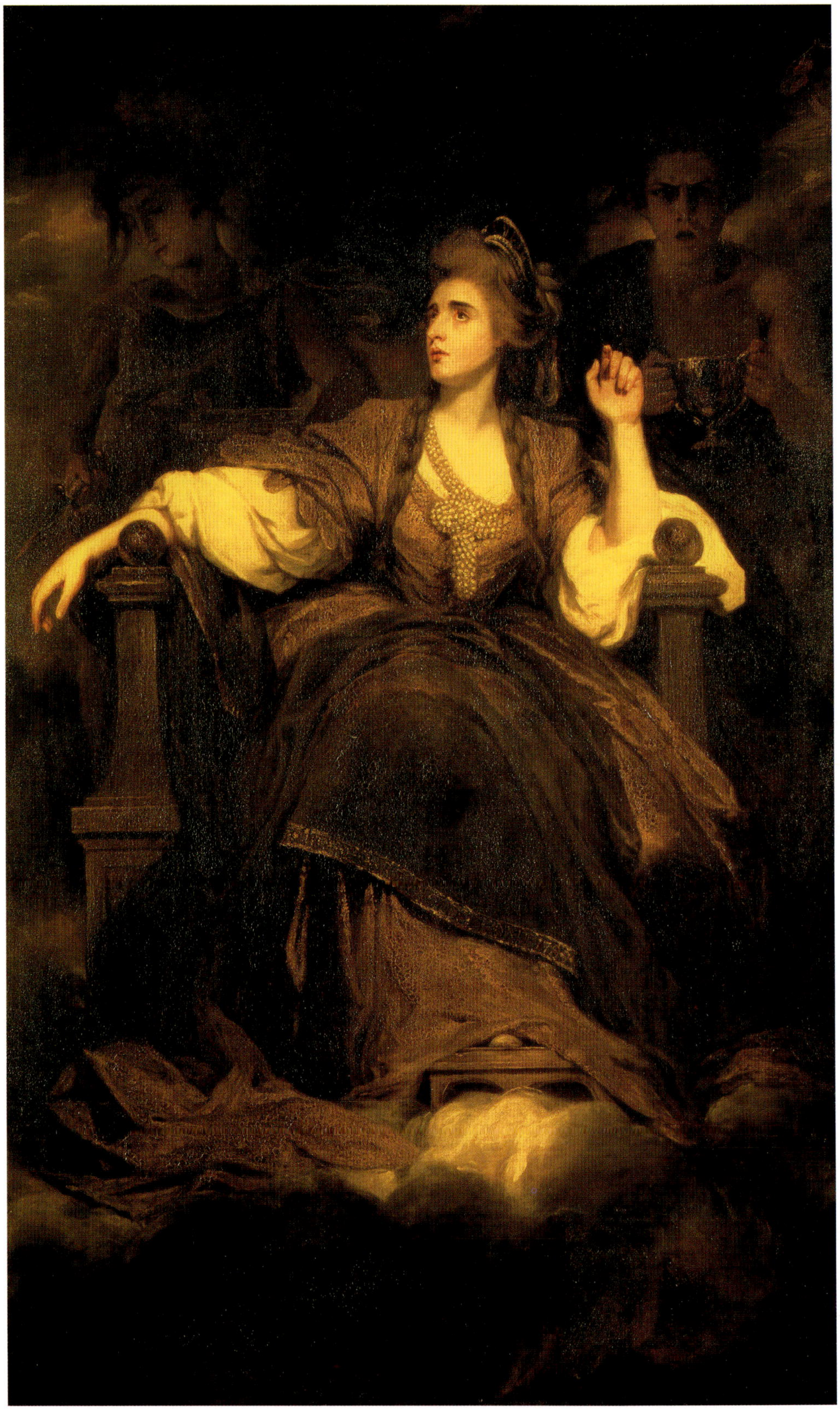

countenance' is especially remarkable in his portrait of *Mrs. Jens Wolff* (Plate 29), begun some years before it was shown at the Royal Academy in 1815. The pose of Reynolds' *Sarah Siddons as The Tragic Muse* is taken from the figure of Isaiah on the ceiling of the Sistine Chapel and the figures behind are copied from the other prophets and sibyls. *Mrs. Jens Wolff* is almost in the pose of the Erythraean Sibyl, which is directly opposite Isiah on the ceiling, and looks at a book of engravings open at a plate of the Delphic Sibyl which, if the analogy is to be continued, is next to Isaiah. It was perhaps inevitable that Reynolds should use a Michaelangelo pose to flatter Mrs Siddons, 'Ascend your undisputed throne, and graciously bestow on me some grand Idea of the Tragick Muse', he said to her, and no doubt the Michaelangelo references in the portrait of Mrs Wolff are partly a personal tribute as well.

Mrs Wolff was the wife of the Danish Consul in London, who lived in Battersea in a house called Sherwood Lodge. Robert Smirke was commissioned to build a sculpture gallery onto the house and Jens Wolff filled it with casts of antique statues. Part of the gallery is just visible in the picture but Mrs Wolff is protected from it by a screen. This dividing screen and perhaps even the statue, which appears to be a Niobe, seem to be references to Mrs Wolff's separation from her husband which took place in 1810, whilst the picture was being painted. Lawrence took an unusual amount of trouble over the portrait; there are at least two drawings for it, one showing Mrs Wolff in profile to the right rather than to the left, and the posthumous sales included a large scale drawing on canvas. Lawrence's relationship with Mrs Wolff was perhaps the most satisfactory that he ever had and his letters to her, especially the ones from Rome, are the most passionate that survive from him. As well as being a colour foil to the brilliantly executed white satin dress, the full blown rose over her heart might well be a reference to this

Fig 8 **Sarah Siddons as the Tragic Muse**
Sir Joshua Reynolds, 1789
Dulwich Picture Gallery, London

relationship, and by referring to Michaelangelo through his hero Reynolds, Lawrence is showing Mrs Wolff how highly he thinks of her. The expressive qualities of Lawrence's portraiture are combined with his sublime yearnings in this portrait of Mrs Wolff. There is also a certain amount of self-indulgent Romantic theatricality, or theatrical romance, as well as a virtuoso display of technique. All these qualities are to be found in the Waterloo Gallery portraits, and on an immense scale.

The specific impetus for the Waterloo Gallery pictures seems to have come from Lady Anne Barnard. The King of Prussia and the Emperor of Russia were due to visit England in 1814 and she suggested a scheme to commemorate the allied victory over Napoleon. Her ideas were changeable but she seems to have envisaged two large group portraits, one showing the Prince Regent being thanked by Louis XVIII for delivering France from Bonaparte, the other showing the Eastern Monarchs of Austria, Russia and Prussia and their generals. Another scheme, suggested by Lord Charles Stewart, Castlereagh's brother and newly appointed ambassador to Vienna, was for Lawrence to go out to Vienna and paint the victors during the Peace Congress. The scheme grew as the Prince Regent began to commission portraits, not only of the Emperor of Russia and the King of Prussia, but also of Generals Platov and Blücher whilst they were in London. The original idea of the two groups was subsequently dropped however and Lawrence began the series of thirty portraits that hangs in the Waterloo Chamber. Sir Jeffrey Wyattville's estimate, in the late 1820s, for a chamber to be built over the old Horn Court at Windsor is the first specific reference to a room to house all the portraits and they were exhibited as a group for the first time in 1830, after Lawrence's death and after those that remained unfinished had been completed by his studio. The present neo-gothic hall was completed in the 1830s. Overbearing and inappropriate, this rather tasteless 'Valhalla' is redeemed only because of Lawrence's ability to capture individuality of features, expression and personality and expand them into the grandest possible forms. The portraits hang in two rows, the full lengths of monarchs and more important military personnel above the three-quarter lengths of the politicians and lesser generals.

The project rapidly got under way and the first portraits to be completed were all shown at the Royal Academy in 1815. They portrayed *Field Marshall Gebhardt von Blücher* the Prussian General (Plate 31), *Ivanovich, Count Platov*, the Cossack leader (Plate 32), *Clemens Lothar Wenzel, Prince Metternich* the Austrian Foreign Minister (Plate 33) and *Arthur Wellesley, 1st Duke of Wellington* (Plate 28), who dominates the Waterloo Chamber, holding the Sword of State in front of St. Paul's Cathedral.

Lawrence was knighted in 1815 in anticipation of his role as artistic ambassador. However, the Hundred Days and Waterloo itself intervened and it was not until 1818 that the mission got under way in Aix-la-Chapelle where the monarchs foregathered before going on to Vienna. Lawrence was to be provided with a special temporary studio but it never arrived and he had to use the town hall, which he politely described as the finest studio he had ever used. Here he completed the portraits of *Alexander I, Emperor of Russia* (Plate 36) and *Frederick William III, King of Prussia* (Plate 37), left unfinished in London four years previously, as well as painting the meek Emperor Francis of Austria.

The success of Lawrence's Winter in Vienna was exceeded only by the success of his Spring in Rome. He was, initially, rather reluctant to go to Italy but the esteem with which he was greeted on all sides soon made him change his mind. Known as *Il Tiziano Inglesi*, Lawrence matched the climax of the Waterloo Chamber portraits. Although the understated and elegant *Joannes, Count Capo D'Istria* (Plate 38) was Lawrence's favourite amongst the smaller portraits, he recognised the triumph of his portrait of *Pope Pius VII* (Plate 40). The brilliance of the technique, the breadth of the composition and the depth of characterisation have parallels in many of the other portraits in the series but in none of the others are these elements combined to such dazzling effect.

Although Lawrence had been the ideal courtier from the age of five and was the humblest and most modest of men, he was not above seeing a parallel between his own artistic position and the

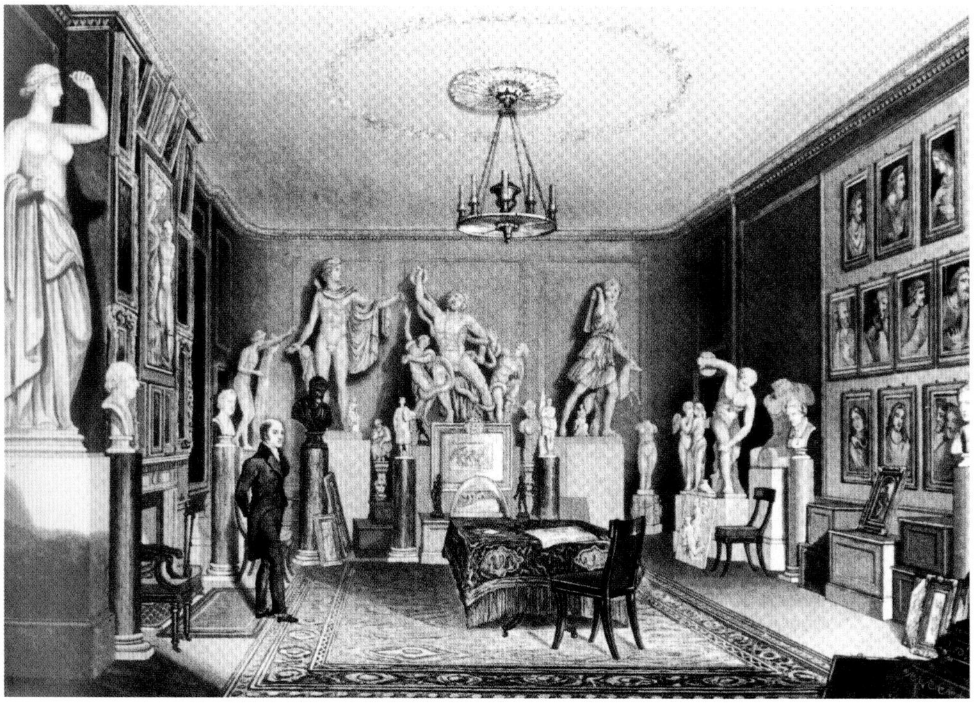

Fig 9 **Thomas Lawrence's sitting room at 65 Russell Square, London.**

position of the Pope as guardian of the art of the past. In the top left-hand corner of the portrait of the Pope the *Laocoon* and the *Apollo Belvedere*, recently returned from their sojourn in the Musée Napoleon, stand in front of Pius VII's new addition to the Vatican Museums. They represent Pius' ultimate triumph over Napoleon, the physical accoutrements of everyday life at the Vatican and the Pope's spiritual curatorial position. The print of Lawrence in his own sitting room (Fig. 9) shows him surrounded by masterpieces from the past, including casts of the *Laocoon* and the *Apollo Belvedere* as well as a wall full of drawings by Leonardo and a small painting by Raphael. He saw these as complementing his position as head of the British School of Art. The fact that he rarely quoted directly from the art of the past in his portraits is irrelevant; it was his duty to make the very best available for study and it was the business of the individual artist whether or not the example of the very best was followed.

His deep admiration of artists like Bonnington, and Turner, who he thought was the only artist who could do justice to the Roman Campagna; his active encouragement of many young artists such as Etty and Eastlake; his support of artists like Blake, from whom he bought two drawings, and Fuseli, from whom he bought a picture annually for many years, show Lawrence's active concern for the arts in England. He was instrumental in the purchase of the Elgin Marbles in 1816 and of the Angerstein pictures to form the National Gallery in 1824. He wanted his collection of drawings to be made into a national collection and had he been less generous in his support of contemporary art there would have been no need for their dispersal — the sum released only just covered his debts. Lawrence did perhaps more than anyone to form our present-day attitudes of awe and reverence towards art galleries and public collections.

Lawrence's interest in contemporary art on the continent is more difficult to pinpoint. His technique was wondered at across Europe but nobody seemed capable of copying it. Like Constable's *Hay Wain* in 1824, Lawrence's *Charles William Lambton* (Plate 46) was admired at the 1827 Salon and his influence is discernible if not especially obvious in Delacroix's *Baron Schwiter* in the National Gallery, London. Apart from Canova, Lawrence's one close foreign artist friend was Baron Gérard who annoyed him initially because he was paid twice Lawrence's fee for his mediocre portraits of the allied sovereigns. The relationship developed, however, during the 1820s; Lawrence painted Gérard's portrait and Gérard helped to find drawings for Lawrence's collection. Lawrence's last Address includes a long tribute to a contemporary German artist, Friedrick Overbeck, whose linear style Lawrence praised with his customary abandon and one of whose cartoons for the frescoes in the Villa Massimo he owned.

Géricault was also admired by Lawrence; he owned two of his sketchbooks and the hussar in the

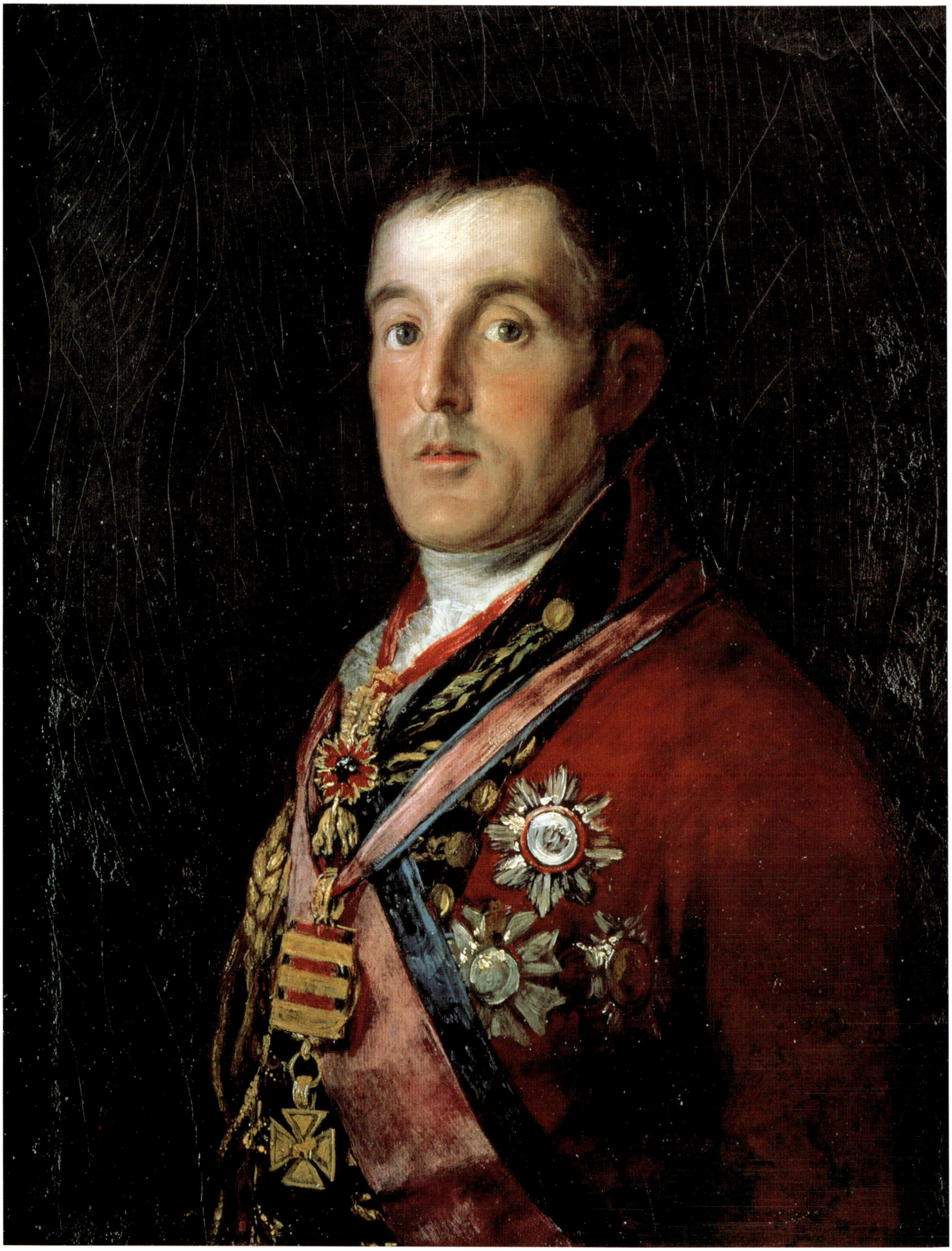

background of the portrait of *Field Marshall Gebhardt von Blücher* is evidently inspired by the French artist's early military portraits which Lawrence would have seen during his trip to Paris in 1815. Gericault and Lawrence shared an interest in and a commitment to the accurate depiction of the emotions as expressed in the physiognomy and the scientific interest of the Romantics in the reproduction of the intangible. In his portraits of the insane, Gericault was certainly sharing Lawrence's early dictum of 'expressing with truth the human heart in the traits of the countenance'.

The directness of approach to his sitter's personality is ultimately Lawrence's greatest achievement, whether with the intimacy of his earlier portrait of *Robert Stewart, Viscount Castlereagh* (Plate 24) or with the swagger of the one-legged *Lord Anglesey*. It is customary to prefer Goya's portrait of the *Arthur Wellesley, 1st Duke of Wellington* (Fig. 10) to Lawrence's (Plate 27), but how far from the truth is Goya's image. The shell-shocked schoolboy weighed down by meaningless medals is a personal interpretation of the pointlessness of war but with Lawrence's portrait we have a real reflection of the sitter's personality: a totally self-confident soldier of genius who went straight from the playing fields of Eton to the battle-fields of India and Western Europe.

Lawrence's attempt to create a type of portrait that combined a slightly vague wish to create visions of the historically sublime with his belief in 'expressing with truth the human heart in the traits of the countenance' was bound to end in compromise, with the historically sublime taking second place. However, the fact that the compromise was a triumphant success is the measure of Lawrence's greatness.

Fig 10 **Portrait of Arthur Wellesley, 1st Duke of Wellington** (1769-1852)
Francisco Goya (1746-1828) 1812-14
National Gallery, London

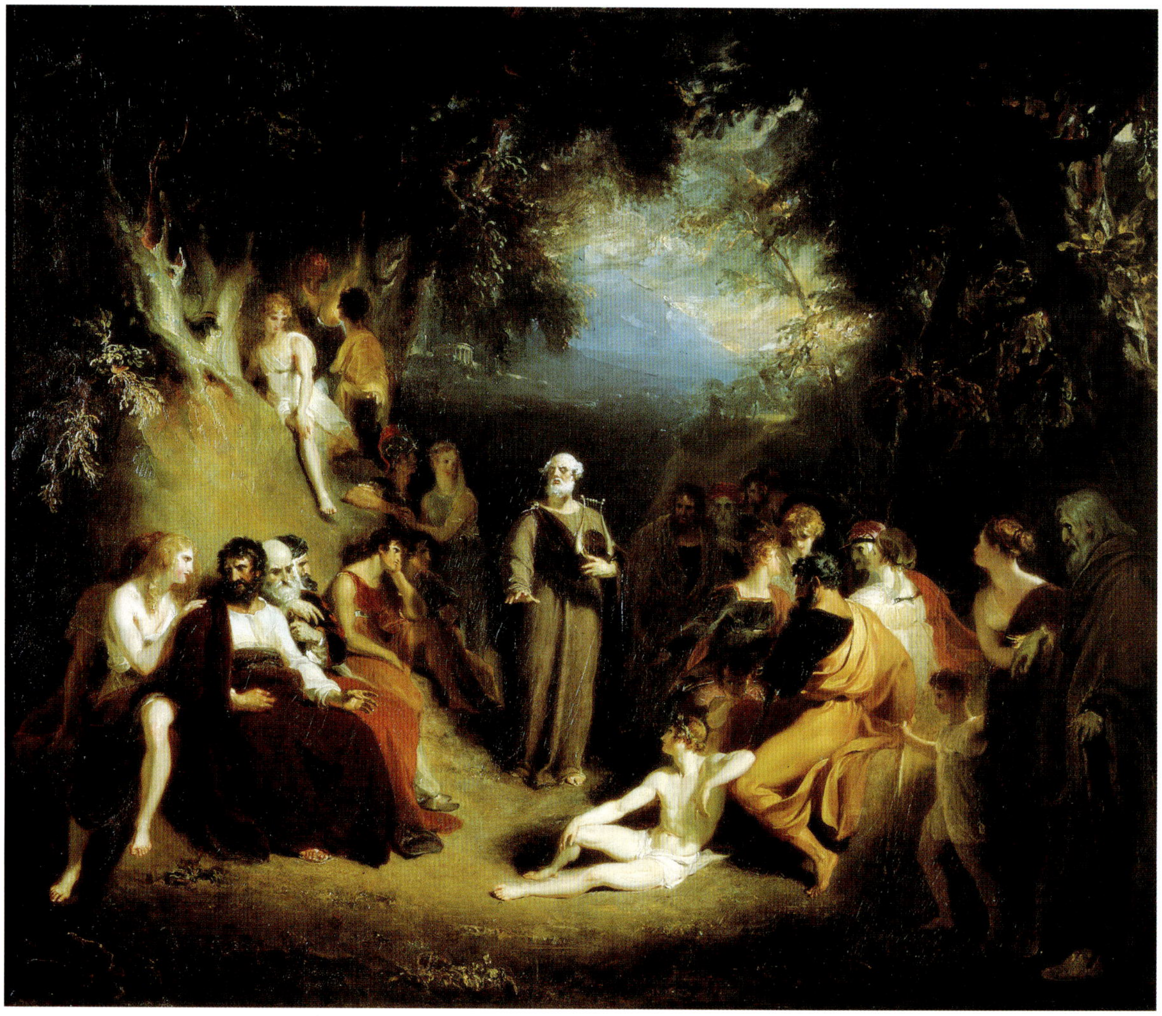

1 **Homer Reciting his Poems**
Canvas $37\frac{1}{2}$ x $43\frac{1}{2}$ in. Begun in 1788,
1791 RA(180)
Tate Britain, London.

Commissioned by Richard Payne Knight in 1788. The naked youth in the foreground was modelled from Lawrence's boxer friend Jackson who also posed for the body of Rolla.

2 **Martha Carr** (born *c.* 1757) (right)
Canvas 30 x 25 in. *c.* 1789
Museo del Prado, Madrid

Miss Carr was the daughter of William Carr, an Irishman who had moved to London, where he lived at Parson's Green until 1800 before selling his house to one Mrs Fitzherbert. This is a probable marriage portrait commemorating her wedding in 1789 to Thomas Chinnall Porter. A photograph taken before restoration reveals that the portrait seems to have been originally presented in an oval format.

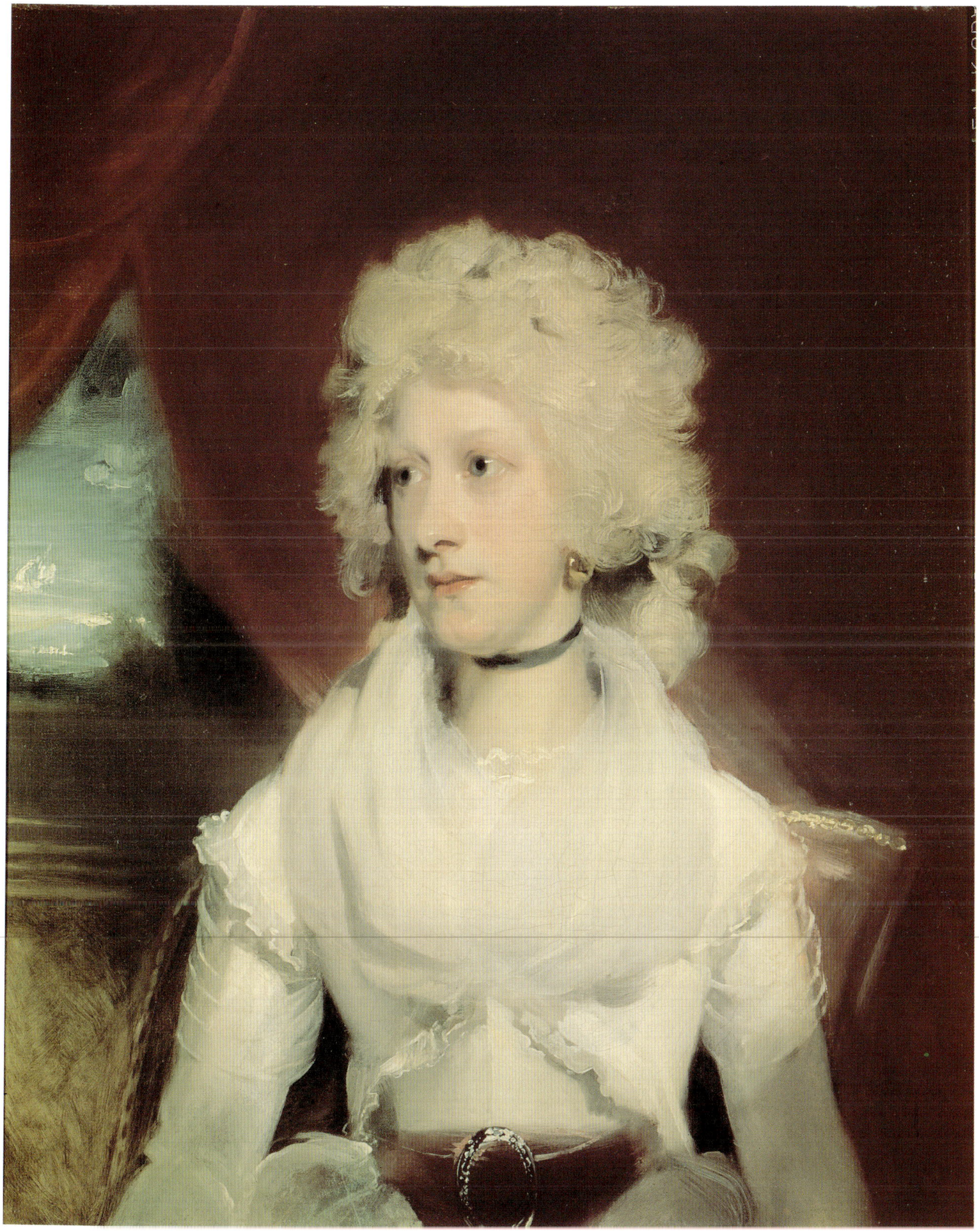

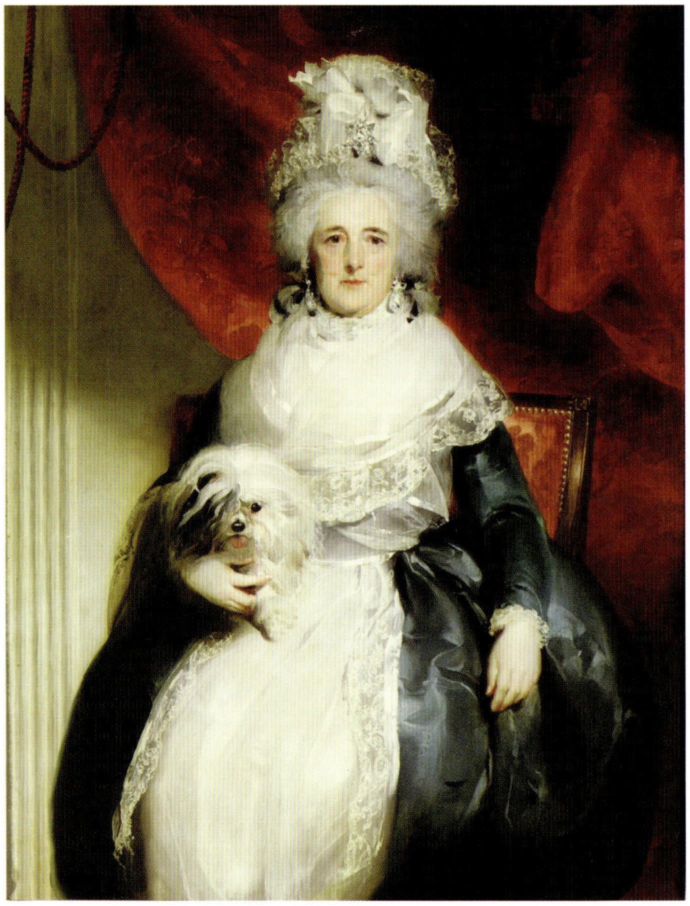

3 **Susanna, Countess of Oxford** (1728-1804)
Canvas 50 x 40 in. 1790
Fyvie Castle, Grampian (The National Trust for Scotland).

The sitter was the daughter of William Archer of Welford, Berkshire. She married the 4th Earl of Oxford in 1751. The imposing figure is softened by the inclusion of the sitter's pet dog.

4 **Queen Charlotte** (1744-1818) (right)
Canvas 94¼ x 58 in. 1790 RA (100)
National Gallery, London.

Charlotte Sophia was the youngest daughter of the 3rd Duke of Mecklenburg-Strelitz and an outsider among the candidates for George III's hand in 1760; she married him in 1761 and was a 'model wife' for almost sixty years. Apart from her children – she had fifteen – her main interest was in Botany although she was famous, perhaps unfairly so, for her passion for jewels.

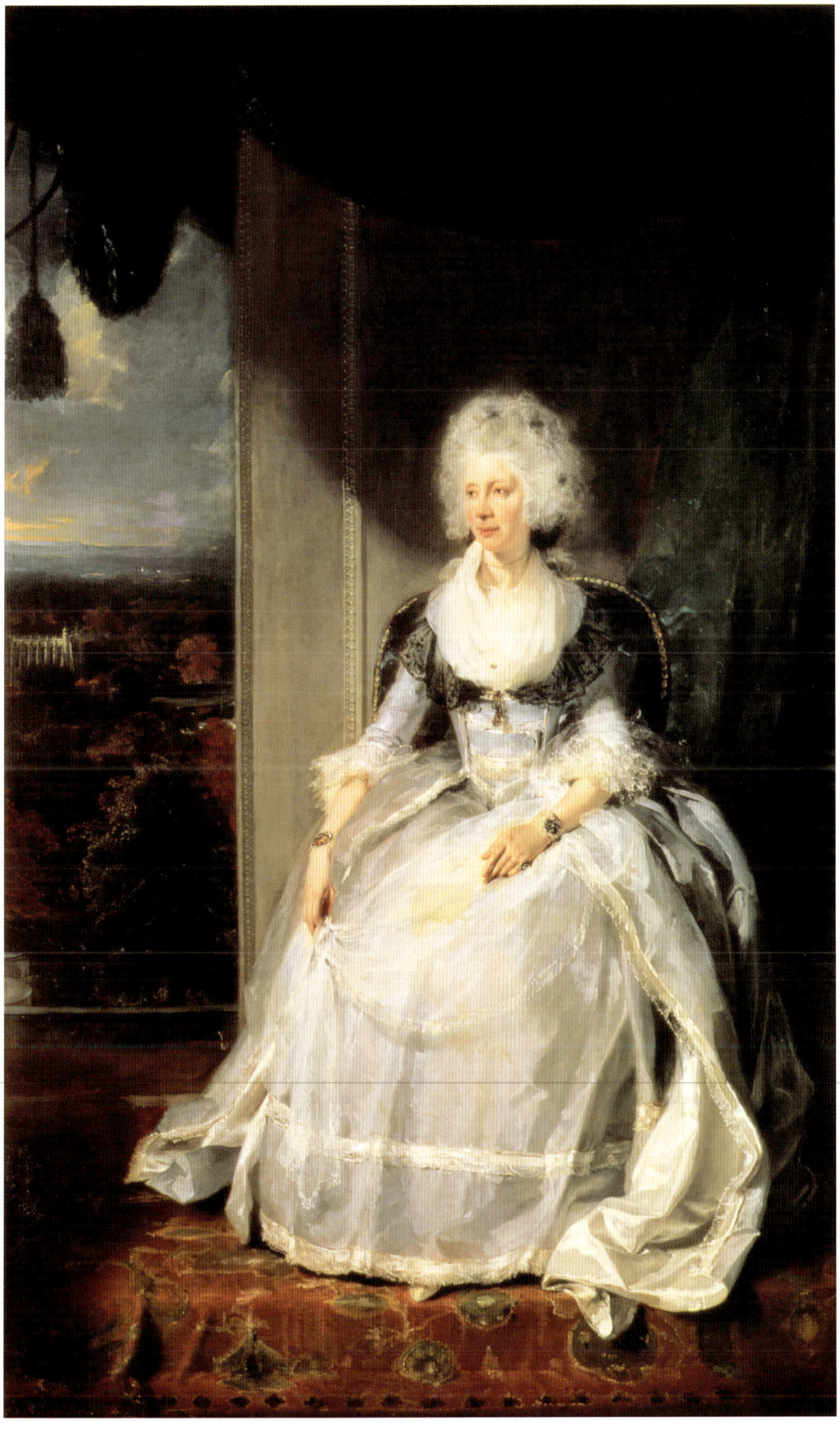

5 **Elizabeth Farren** (1759-1829)
Canvas $93\frac{3}{4}$ x 58 in. 1790 RA (171)
Metropolitan Museum of Art, New York.

Daughter of the actor George Farren, who came from a Huguenot family who had settled in Dublin, actress Elizabeth Farren made her name in comedy roles and became the star of Drury Lane. She was called the Queen of Comedy by Horace Walpole, and as a comedienne specialising in 'fine ladies' her only rival on the British stage was Frances Abington.

Her stage career began before 1774 and ended with a performance in *The School for Scandal* of her best known part, Lady Teazel, in 1797, three weeks before her marriage to the 12th Earl of Derby.

Exhibited at the Royal Academy in the vicinity of Reynolds' traditional portrait of Mrs Billington, the star of Covent Garden, portrayed as St Cecilia, the contemporary and unacademic style of the Lawrence was all the more provocative. The actress, influenced by her friends, felt that she looked too thin but the press were enamoured, with the *Public Advertiser* enthusing, 'completely Elizabeth Farren; arch, careless, spirited and engaging.'

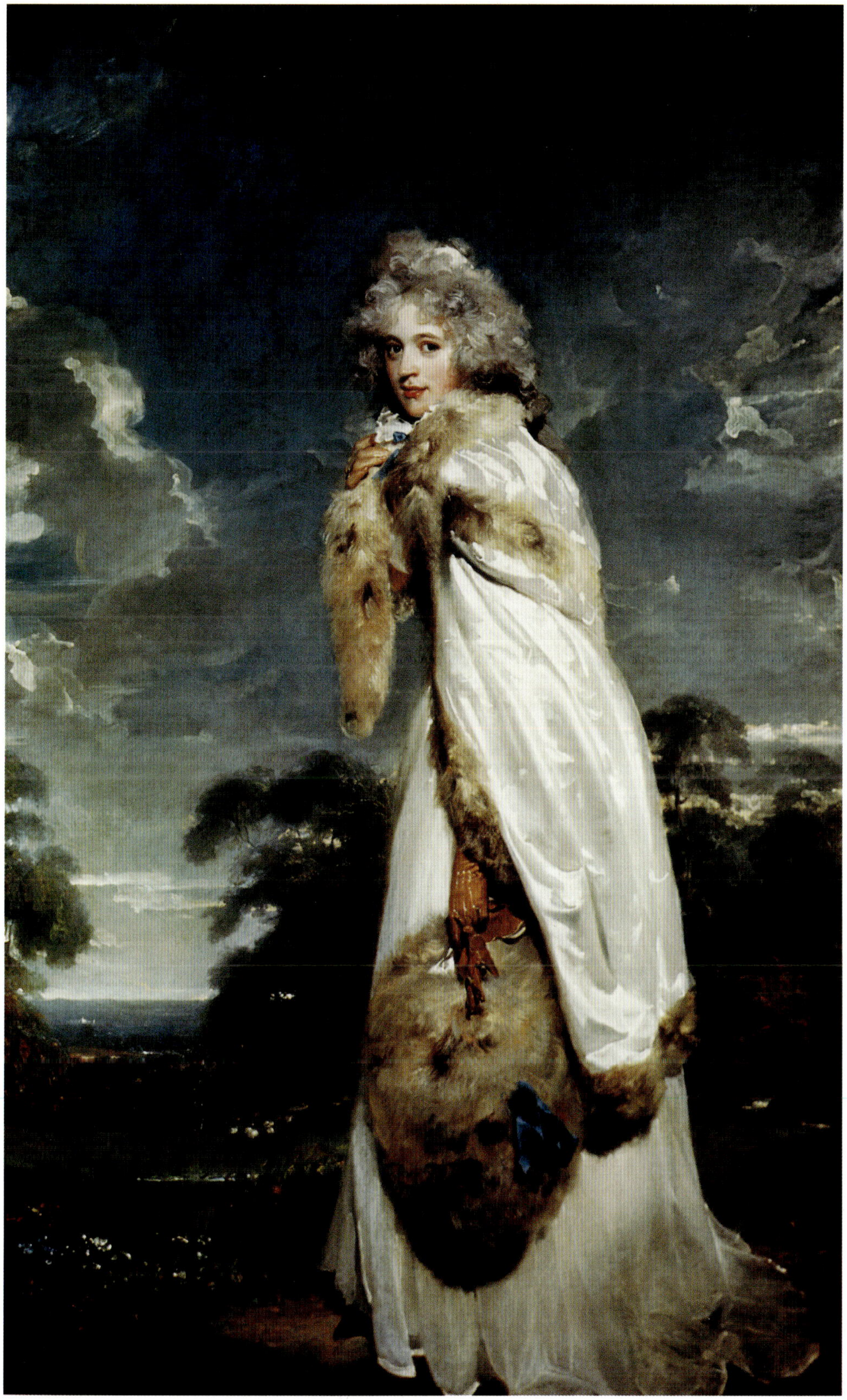

6 **Arthur Atherley, MP** (1772-1844)
Canvas 49½ x 39½ in. *c.* 1791-2
1792 RA (209)
Los Angeles County Museum of Art, Los Angeles.

Arthur Atherley was the eldest son of Arthur Atherley of Southampton.

One of the most well loved of Lawrence's portraits, this striking picture portrays the young sitter as both elegant and self assured. The portrait was mistaken in a contemporary newspaper for Tom Sheridan, the son of famous dramatist, Richard Brinsley Sheridan.

It is likely that the portrait was painted at around the time Atherley was leaving Eton. He takes his hat off to Eton College Chapel which can be seen to the right of the background. He went up to Trinity College, Cambridge and, a staunch Whig, subsequently became M.P. for Southampton during the three Parliaments 1806-07, 1812-18 and 1831-33.

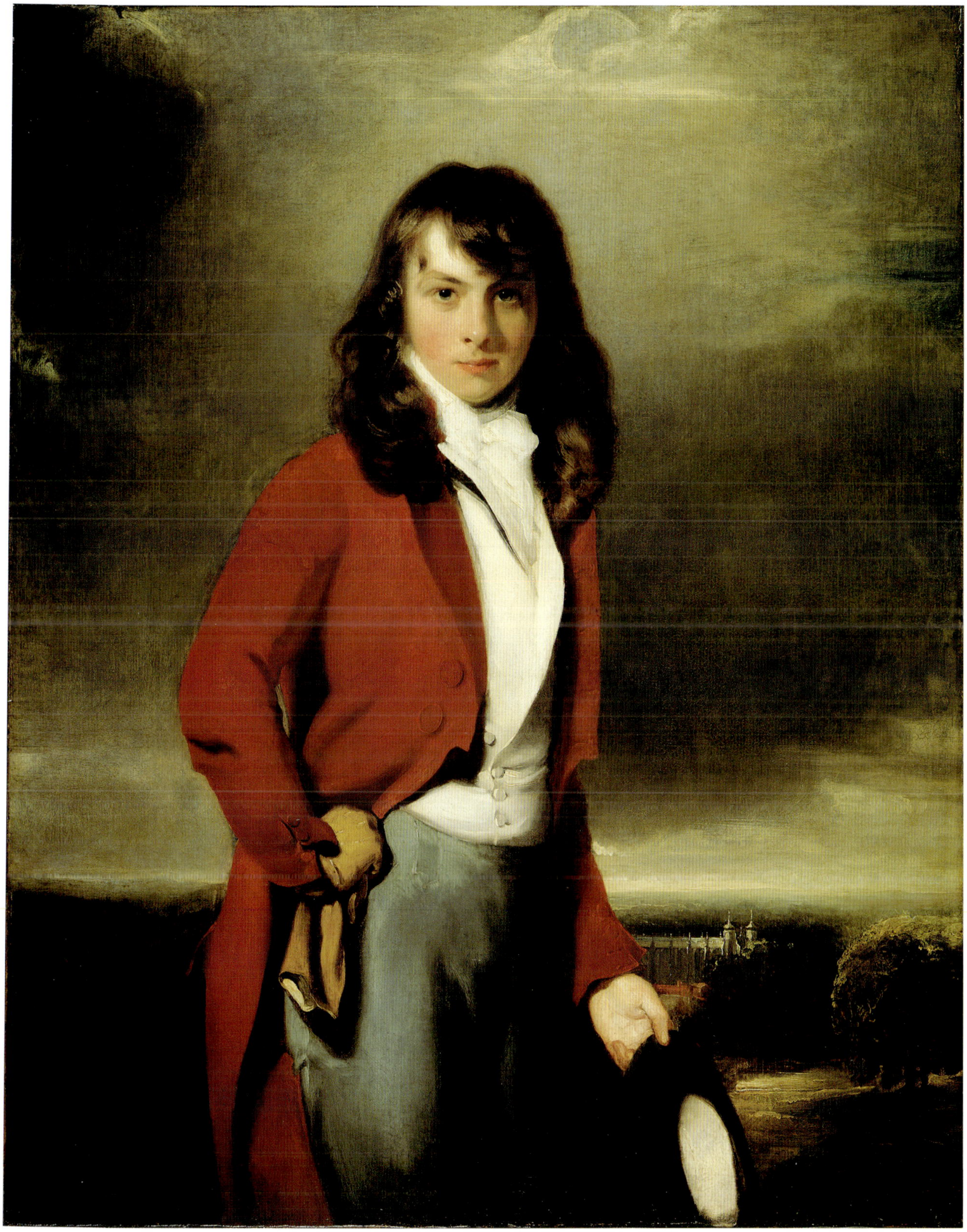

7 **George III** (1738-1820)
Canvas 108½ x 60½ in. RA 1792 (65)
St. Mary's Hall, Coventry.

Although Lawrence was appointed Painter in Ordinary to the King in the same year that this portrait was shown at the Royal Academy, George III does not seem to have liked the image that Lawrence created. He insisted that Lawrence copy Reynolds' state portrait for diplomatic gifts such as that sent with Lord Macartney's mission to the Emperor of China in 1792, and Lawrence and his studio were committed to such humiliating hack work until around 1815. However, versions of this portrait were commissioned from Lawrence in the 1820s by George IV and the City of Liverpool. A three-quarter length portrait of George III, showing him seated, was painted for the Speaker of the House of Commons in 1809.

George III succeeded his grandfather, George II, in 1760.

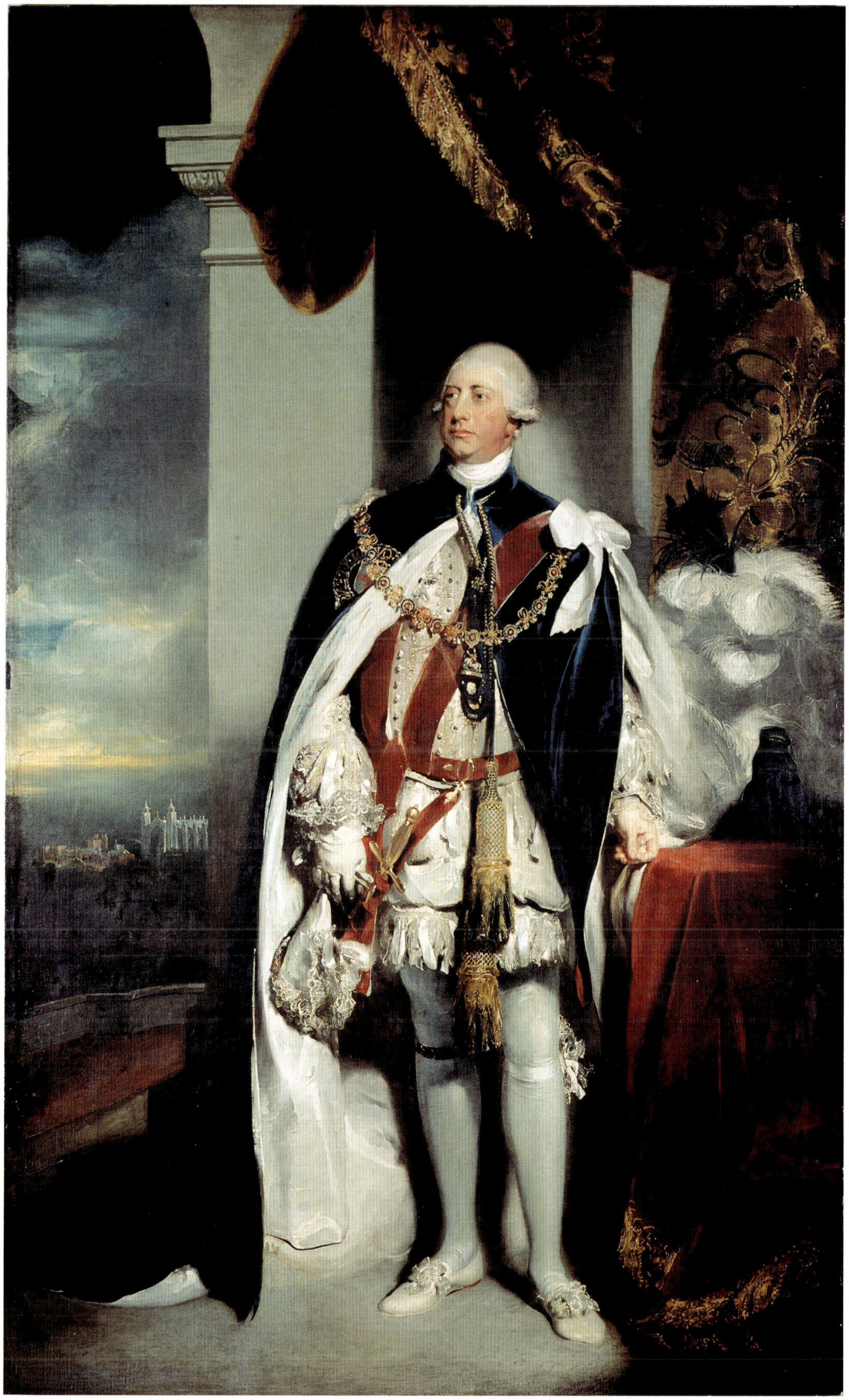

8 **Charles, 1st Earl Grey** (1729-1807)
Canvas 50 x 40 in. 1795 RA(131)
Private collection.

Joseph Collyer's stipple engraving of this portrait was published in 1797 as a money-raising venture for the widows and children of those killed in Earl Grey's West Indian campaigns.

'…A Portrait of Sir Charles Grey K.B., late Commander-in-Chief in the West Indies; from a capital picture painted by Mr. Lawrence, R.A., Portrait Painter in Ordinary to his Majesty; engraved in a most finished style by Mr. Joseph Collyer, Engraver to her Majesty; and published by the proprietor, W. Austin, Drawing-Master, Turnham Green. Proof prints, two guineas; prints, one guinea each.

'Mr. Austin respectfully solicits the patronage of the public to an undertaking he has the pleasure of submitting to them; the profits of which, he pledges himself, shall be applied to the fund established for the relief of the widows and children of the brave Britons who have lost their lives in their country's cause, in the expedition under the joint command of those gallant officers, Sir Charles Grey K.B. and Vice-Admiral Sir J. Jervis K.B. Mr. Austin doubts not, from the characteristic benevolence of the English nation, of being enabled to add to the increase of a fund founded on such noble principles. And it must be a peculiar gratification to every Briton to be in possession of a portrait of an officer, to whose bravery and skill his country is so essentially indebted…'.

Charles Grey was the second surviving son of Sir Henry Grey Bt. He joined the army as an ensign in 1748 and served in various continental campaigns before and during the Seven Years War. He had a remarkably successful record during the American Rebellion and was appointed Commander-in-Chief of the army just as the war ended. In 1793-4 he fought the French in the West Indies with the future Earl St. Vincent and was made a general and Privy Councillor in November 1794. He was made 1st Baron Grey de Howick in 1801 and Earl Grey in 1806.

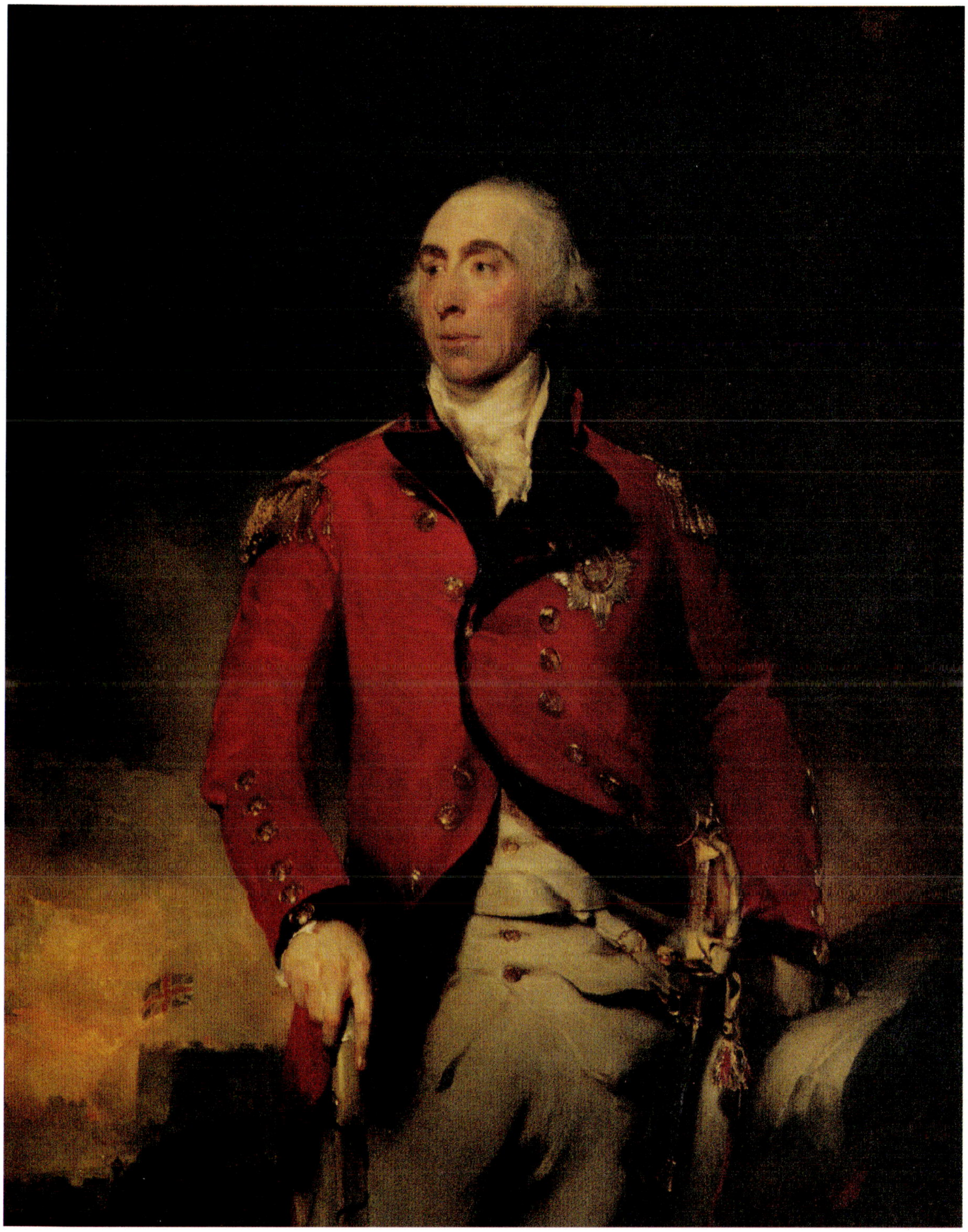

9 **Sarah Goodin Moulton ('Pinkie')** (1783-95)
Canvas 57 x 39 in. RA 1795 (75)
Henry E. Huntington Library and Art Gallery,
San Marino, California.

Judith Barrett, the sitter's maternal grandmother, wrote to her niece, Elizabeth Barrett Williams, on 16 November 1793; living in St. James's, Jamaica, she was anxious to have some reminder of her favourite grandchild, nicknamed Pinkie (or Pinkey), who had left the West Indies for England earlier in the year.

'I became every day more desirous to see my dear little Pinkey; but as I cannot gratify myself with the Original, I must beg favor of You to have her picture drawn at full Length by one of the best Masters in an easy Careless attitude. As your Taste and Judg'ment cannot be excell'd, I leave her Dress to You – You will therefore be so kind as to inform me by the first pacquet after you receive this, what the Amount will be, and I will get a Bill and send You as soon as possible – I shall expect it out as soon as the paint is well dried and Seasoned – Let the frame be handsome and neat'.

Pinkie, who was the aunt of poet Elizabeth Barrett Browning, died on 23 April 1795. The picture was never sent to Jamaica but remained with the family in England until 1910.

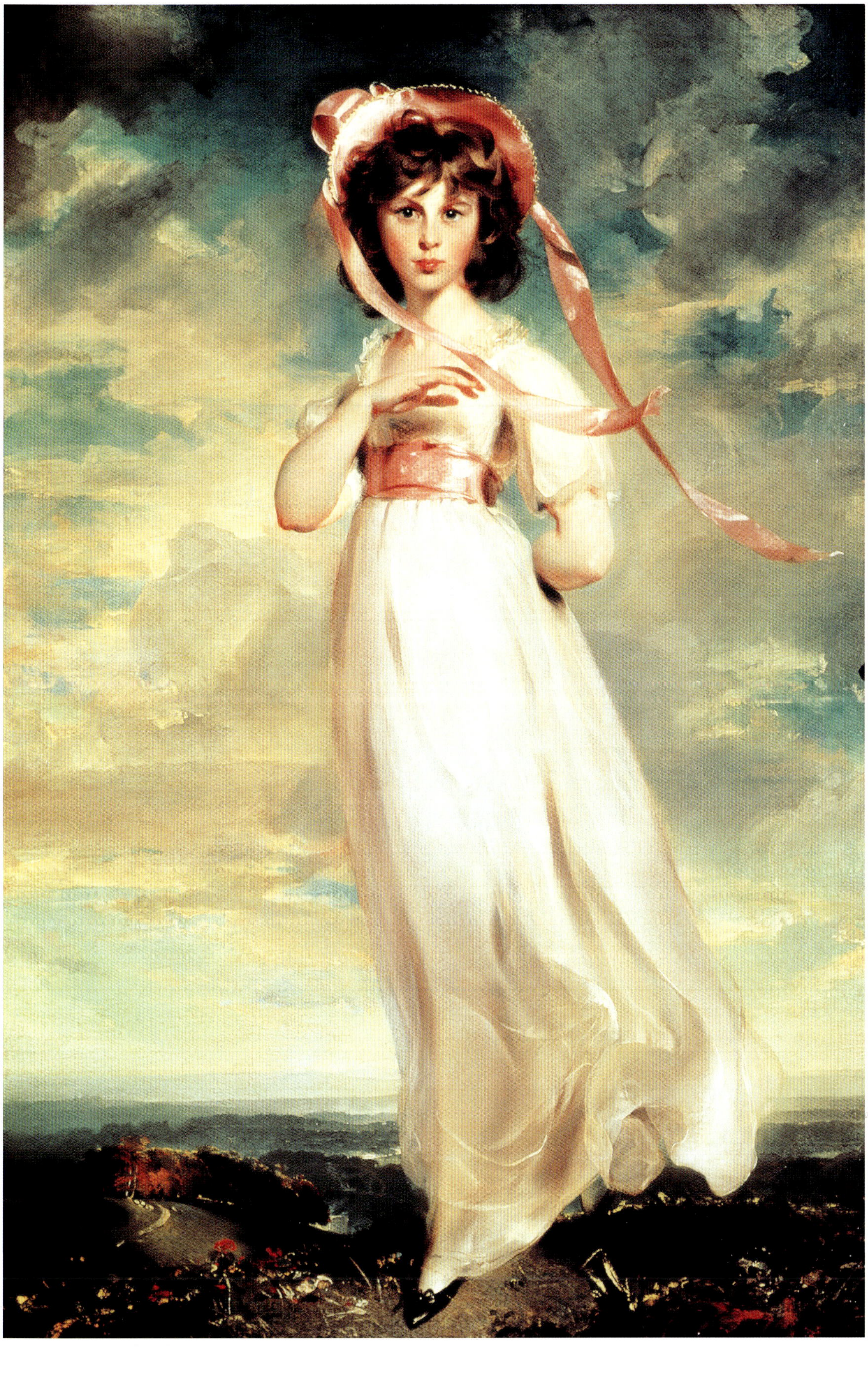

10 **Joseph Farington, RA** (1747-1821)
Canvas 29 x 24 in. 1795
1796 RA (164)
Messrs. P & D. Colnaghi and Co. Ltd., London

Joseph Farington was, from about 1794 until his death, Lawrence's closest friend and advisor, and indeed something of a father substitute. The Lawrence papers in the Royal Academy include several hundred letters to and from Farington.

Farington, a painter and dramatist, became a full Royal Academician in 1785 and, in the early nineteenth century, was probably more influential in artistic matters than Benjamin West, the President. He was an accomplished landscape artist and his diary is the most informative document on artistic life in England in the late eighteenth and early nineteenth centuries.

Sitting for this picture, Farington noted on 7 May, 1794, 'He drew my portrait with black chalk on the canvass which employed him near 2 hours. He did not use colour today. This is his mode of beginning'.

The portrait, in which the sitter appears as if captured, unawares, in motion, stepping in from the right of the frame, has a theatrical quality common to many of Lawrence's works.

A second portrait of Farington was painted by Lawrence in 1808. Whilst this portrait was being painted Farington was endeavouring to sort out Lawrence's financial problems. Lawrence had no head for business. He was saved from financial ruin by the the good offices of his banker, Thomas Coutts, and other wealthy patrons who moved in banking circles.

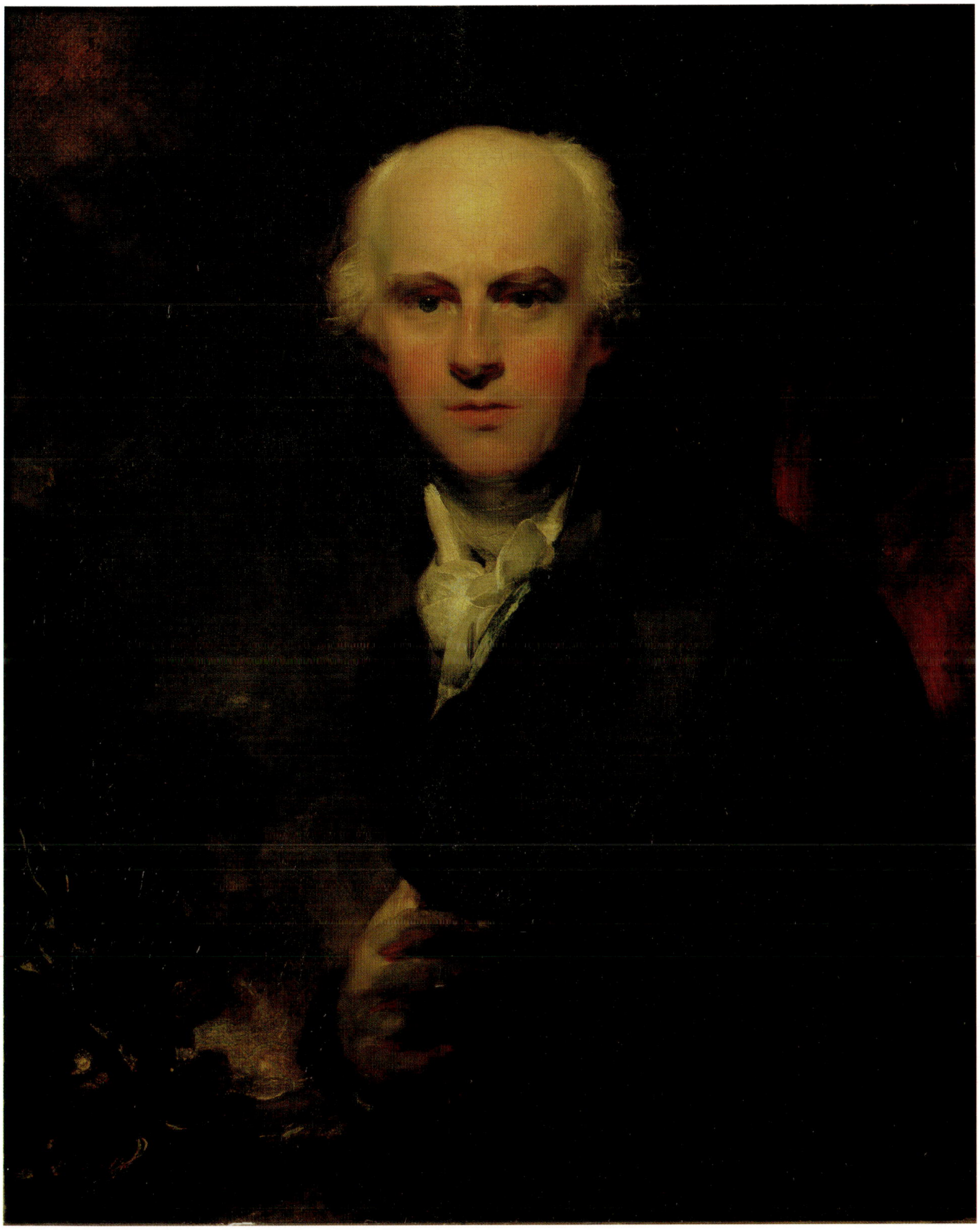

11 **Henry Cecil, 10th Earl of Exeter, later 1st Marquess, with His Wife Sarah, Countess of Exeter; and Daughter, Lady Sophia**
Canvas 86 x 57 in. 1796
RA 1797 (74)
The Burghley House Collection

In 1791, Henry Cecil (1743-1804), nephew of the 9th Earl of Exeter and his heir, married Sarah Hoggins (1773-97) – unbeknownst to his family – as his second wife, having divorced his first wife the same year. Sarah, a village girl from Bolas, Shropshire, pictured here in her new and more noble role, had no idea of his true identity. He succeeded his uncle, two years later, as Earl of Essex and was in 1810 elevated to the rank of Marquess.

The group portrait also includes the Countess' daughter, Lady Sophia Cecil (1792-1823). The Countess herself, however, died in January 1797, shortly before the picture was shown at the Royal Academy. Despite receiving praise, the work came in for criticism from *The Monthly Mirror*, who deemed it 'a good picture on the whole; the nobleman is a dignified figure, but the affected style of this artist is too strongly apparent in the lady and child'. This was not a new criticism for Lawrence, whose style continued to be considered 'affetuoso' by the likes of Constable as late as the 1820s. Lawrence was certainly theatrical, and he was well aware of the Mannerist works of the Italian sixteenth-century, notably Parmigianino. It is from this strain of art that he here gains the exaggeration of the female figures.

In one of his early poems, *The Lord of Burleigh*, Alfred, Lord Tennyson gives a romanticized version of the love affair between Henry Cecil and Sarah Hoggins.

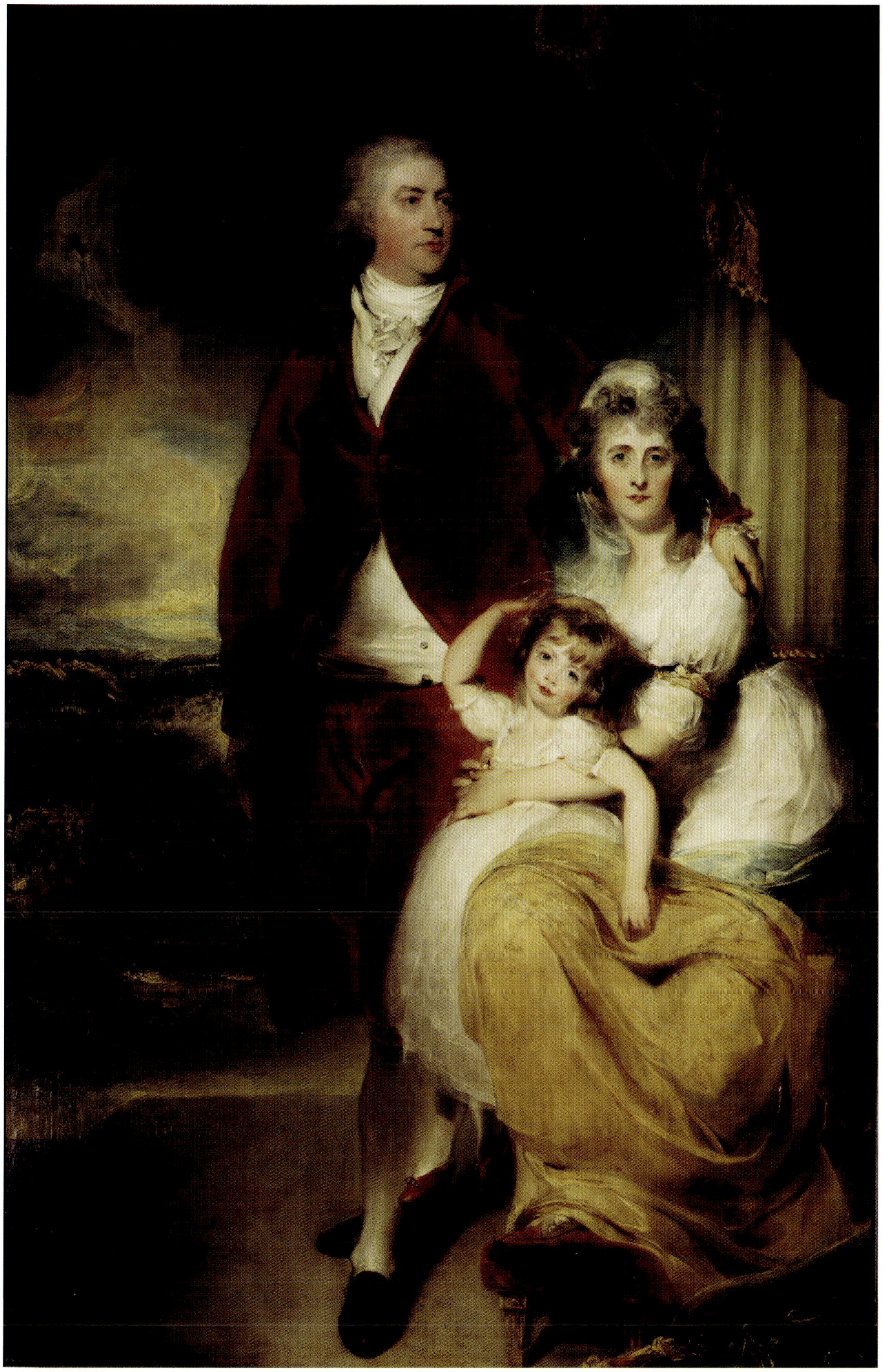

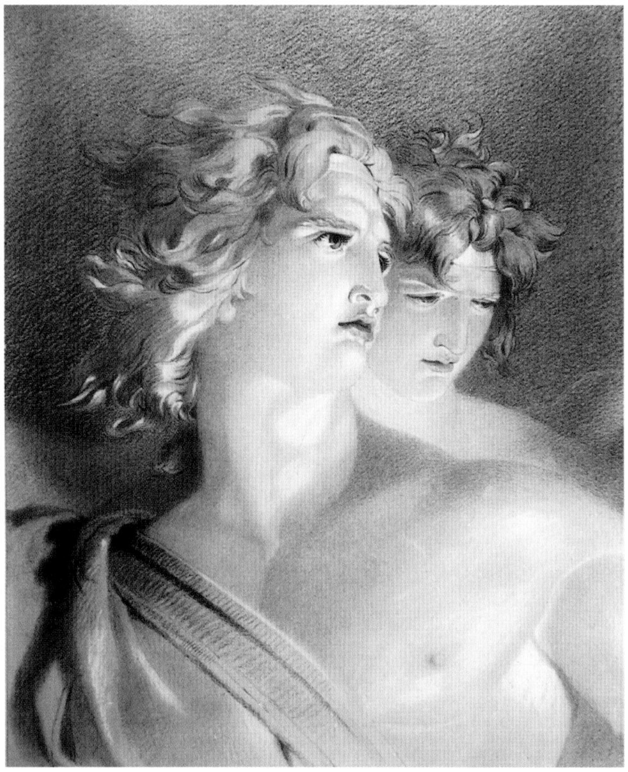

12 **Two Fallen Angels**
Chalk on tinted paper 9½ x 7¾ in.
c. 1797 Private Collection.

Lawrence was an exceptional draughtsman. This beautiful finished drawing relates to the large canvas of *Satan Summoning his Legions*, which illustrates an episode from Milton's *Paradise Lost.* Five drawings for the painting were sold in Lawrence's posthumous sales and several have appeared on the art market since. The 'prettiness' of the protagonist in the drawing is reduced but not eliminated in the final version.

The drawing probably refers to an earlier episode than the related canvas, in which Satan finds Beelzebub beside him, and expresses his defiance of God.

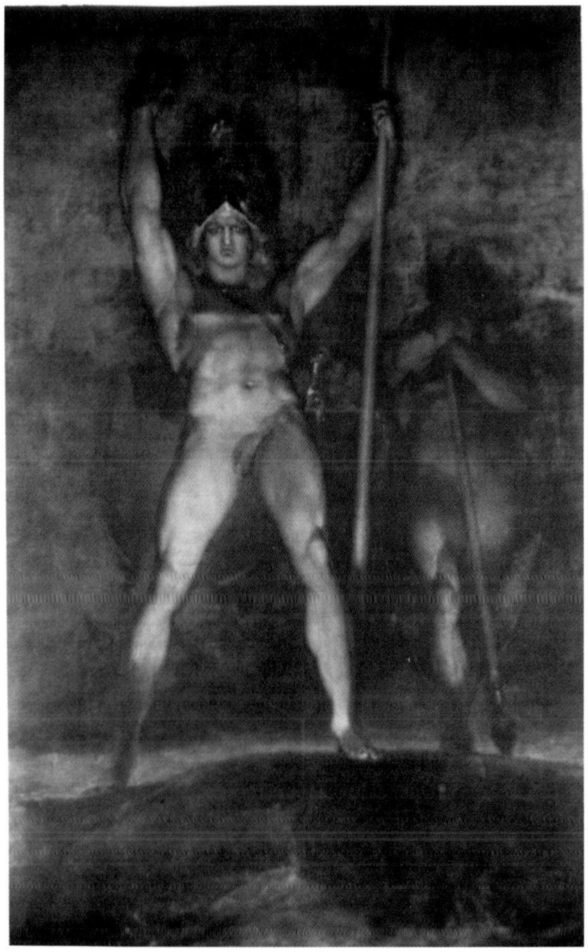

13 **Satan Summoning his Legions**
Canvas 170 x 108 in.
RA 1797 (170) Royal Academy of Fine Arts, London.

Milton, Paradise Lost, Book 1: 'Awake, arise or be for ever fallen'.

Pasquin's criticism of this picture has been previously quoted; a pamphlet entitled 'The Royal Academy, or a Touchstone to the present Exhibition by Anthony Touchstone' deliberately and directly reversed all his vitriolic *bon mots*. A Guide to the Exhibition of the Royal Academy, for 1797, praises Lawrence for transcending his practise of portrait painting.

'170. Satan calling his Legions. Mr. Lawrence has been hitherto chiefly known as a portrait painter. He has in this picture soared into a higher branch of his art with the greatest success. The figure of Satan is truly sublime, and that of the attendant fiend, Beelzebub, is all that the mind of the poet framed. Perhaps somewhat less of distortion in the countenance of the arch fiend would have been more according to Milton's description of him. Upon the whole, this performance must place Mr. Lawrence among the first artists of the English School'.

14 **Sarah Siddons** (1755-1831)
Canvas 30 x 25 in. 1798
Tate Britain, London

Sarah was born in Brecon, Wales, the eldest child of twelve children of the actor Roger Kemble and his wife Sarah Ward. John Philip Kemble, painted by Lawrence on more than one occasion, was her brother. She was a member of her father's theatre company and performed on stage from childhood. She married fellow actor William Siddons in 1773. Lawrence had known her from his boyhood, and on moving to London he became an intimate of the Siddons family.

Playing at the Drury Lane Theatre in 1782 she had sealed her reputation as an unsurpassed tragic actress. She was hugely successful; her rich voice and enormous stage presence enraptured audiences. William Hazlitt wrote that 'passion emanated from her breast as from a shrine, She was tragedy personified'. Her most celebrated role was that of Lady Macbeth, which she first performed in 1785 and also in 1812, at her farewell performance.

Her portrait was painted by Gainsborough, Reynolds and Lawrence. Lawrence first drew her in 1786. This portrait, one of at least two known similar, is somewhat unflattering but revealing of her tragic demeanour. In spite of Lawrence's disastrous relations with her two elder daughters, Sally and Maria, the two remained on good terms. She even asked that he be pallbearer at her funeral. He died, however, before her.

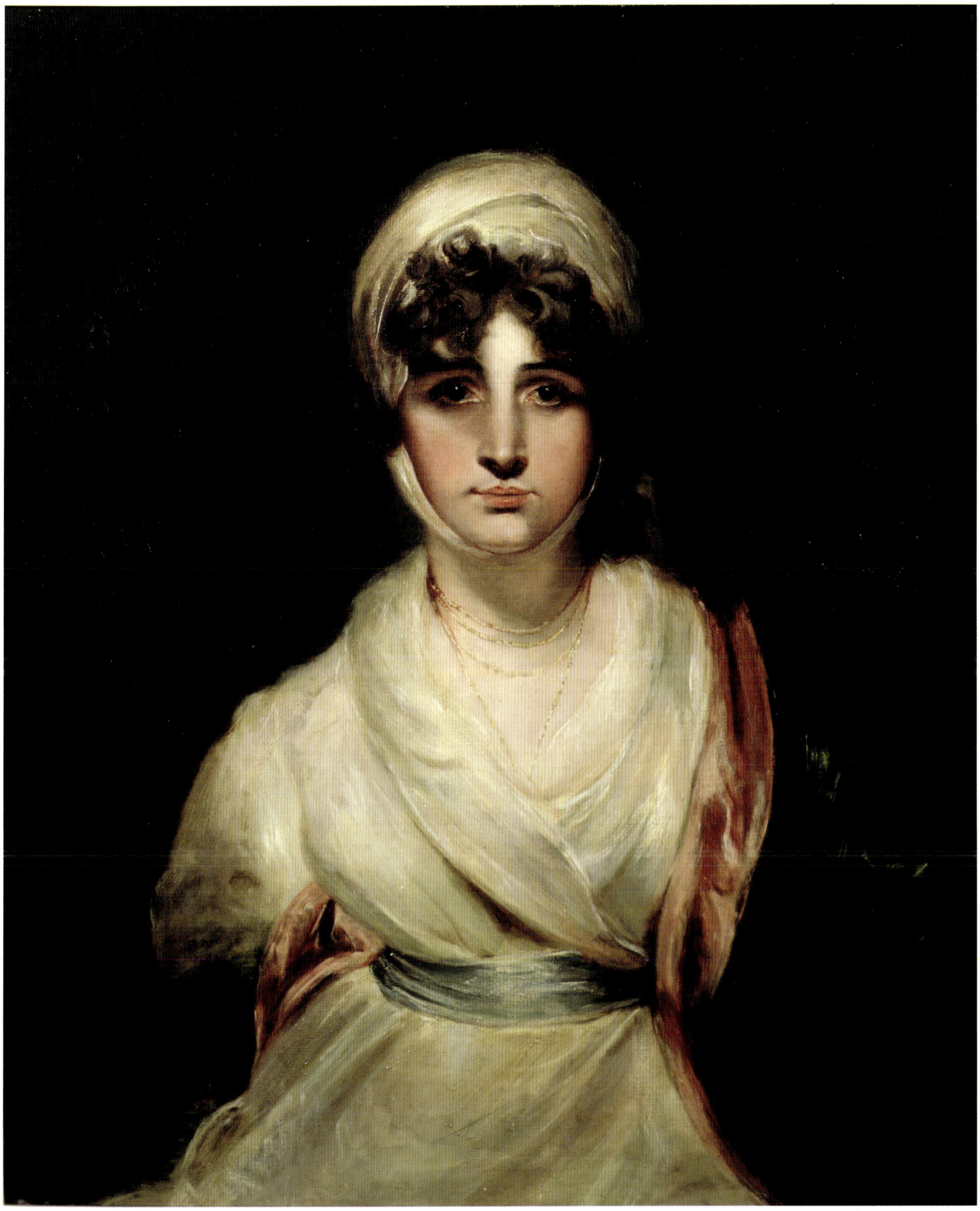

15 **John Philip Kemble as Coriolanus at the Hearth of Tullus Aufidius**
Canvas 113 x 70½ in. RA 1798 (225)
Guildhall Art Gallery, London.

The second of Lawrence's several portraits of Kemble and the first of him in character. Lawrence wrote to Mrs. Ayscough Boucherette whilst he was painting it.

'…I cannot refrain from telling you, that I have nearly finished a sort of half-history picture – Coriolanus at the hearth of Aufidius, which I hope you will like. Indeed, if you do not, you cannot with any justice abuse the painter, for your loitering in Lincolnshire throws me so entirely on my own judgment, that failure seems unavoidable…..'.

Lawrence admired Kemble's performance of Coriolanus and some years later invited Farington to a new production of the play at Covent Garden. The letter is dated 20 December 1811.

'…the Town is fashionably and I had almost said rationally mad after it – I have seen it but once – it will give you the best specimen of Kemble and a fine one of Mrs. Siddons'.

John Philip Kemble (1757-1823) first appeared on the stage in Wolverhampton after an education preparing him for the Catholic priesthood. He made his London debut in 1783 and was appointed stage manager of Drury Lane by Sheridan in 1788. In 1802 he, and his sister Sarah Siddons, moved to Covent Garden. He played Rolla in the first production of Sheridan's adaptation of Kotzebue's play at Drury Lane in 1799, one of the roles in which Lawrence painted him. Having bought a large interest in Covent Garden he quickly rebuilt it after the fire of 1808. His last appearance on stage was again as Coriolanus, in 1817.

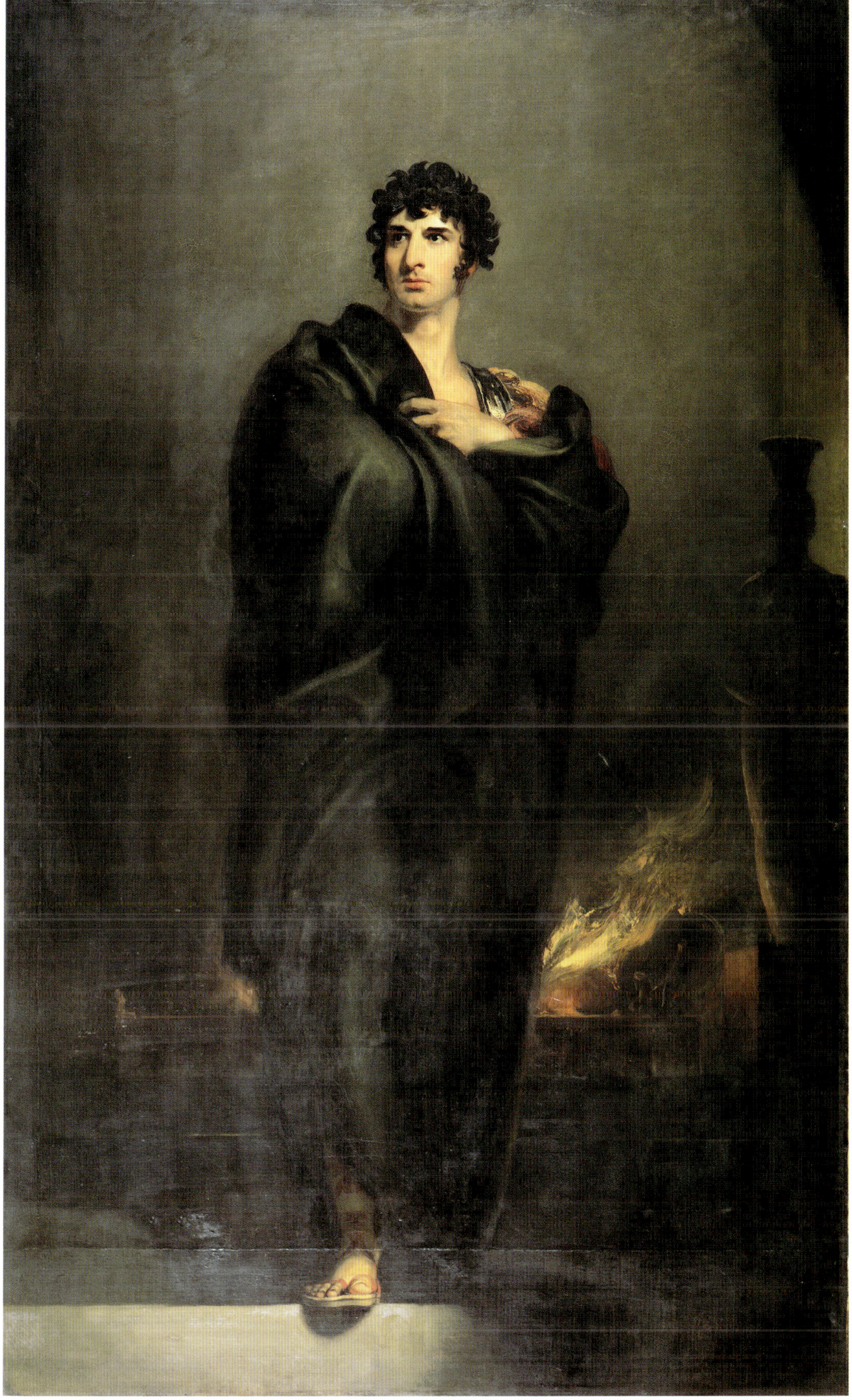

16 **Samuel Lysons, FSA, FRS.** (1763-1819)
Canvas 30 x 25 in. *c.* 1798-9
RA 1799 (137)
Yale Center for British Art, Paul Mellon Collection

Samuel Lysons (1763-1819), an antiquary, was one of Lawrence's close professional friends, along with Joseph Farington. Lysons, the younger son of the Reverend Samuel Lysons, was Keeper of the Tower of London records (1805), Vice-President and Treasurer of the Royal Society (1810) and Antiquary of the Royal Academy. His masterwork was the *Reliquiae Britannico-Romano* (1810-17), and he was responsible for excavating the Roman pavement at Woodchester, Gloucestershire. He also drew up the Lawrence family tree.

A fine pencil drawing of Lysons by Lawrence, possibly a preliminary study for this portrait, is held in the National Portrait Gallery, London. The portrait is notable for the subtle and thoughtful expression of the sitter's face.

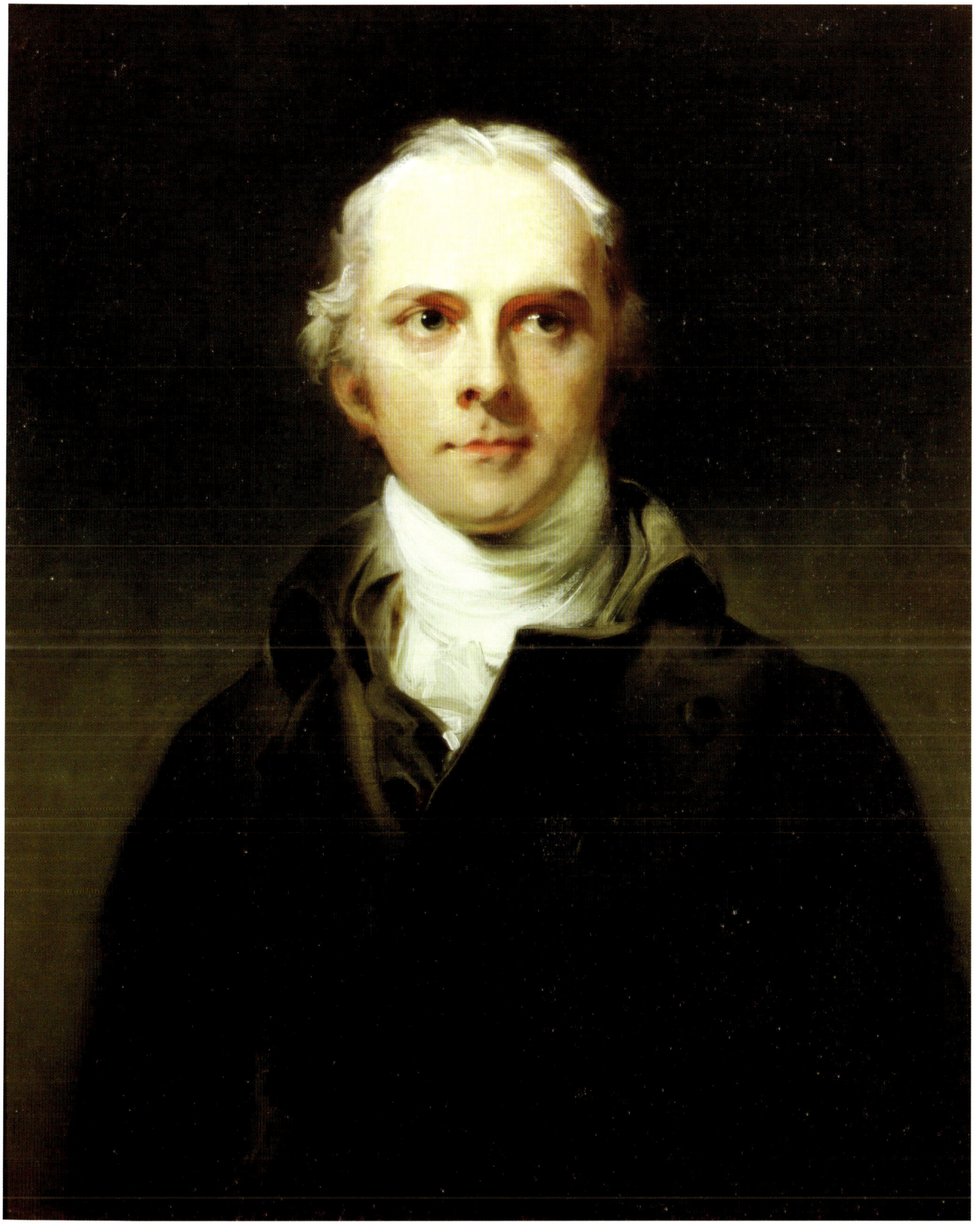

17 **The Children of Ayscoghe Boucherett**
Canvas 76⅜ x 57 in.
c. 1799-1800
RA 1800 (28)
Musée du Louvre, Paris

The M.P. of North Willingham, Lincolnshire, Ayscoghe Boucherett, married Emilia, the step-daughter of the merchant and important collector John Julius Angerstein, in 1790. The Angerstein and Boucherett families were great friends and it was through the Angerstein family that the Bouchereetts came to know Lawrence. He drew and painted many members of both families. Indeed, this painting was known for many years as *The Children of John Angerstein*. Kenneth Garlick's detailed investigations revealed it rather to portray Boucherett's children.

The four children in this group portrait are Emilia Mary (1790-1874), Ayscoghe (1791-1857), Juliana (died 1861) and Maria (1797-1867). This group portrait was subtitled *The Little Orator* in the catalogue of the Royal Academy exhibition of 1800 and in fact the children are portrayed here in striking rhetorical, if not theatrical, poses at odds with their years.

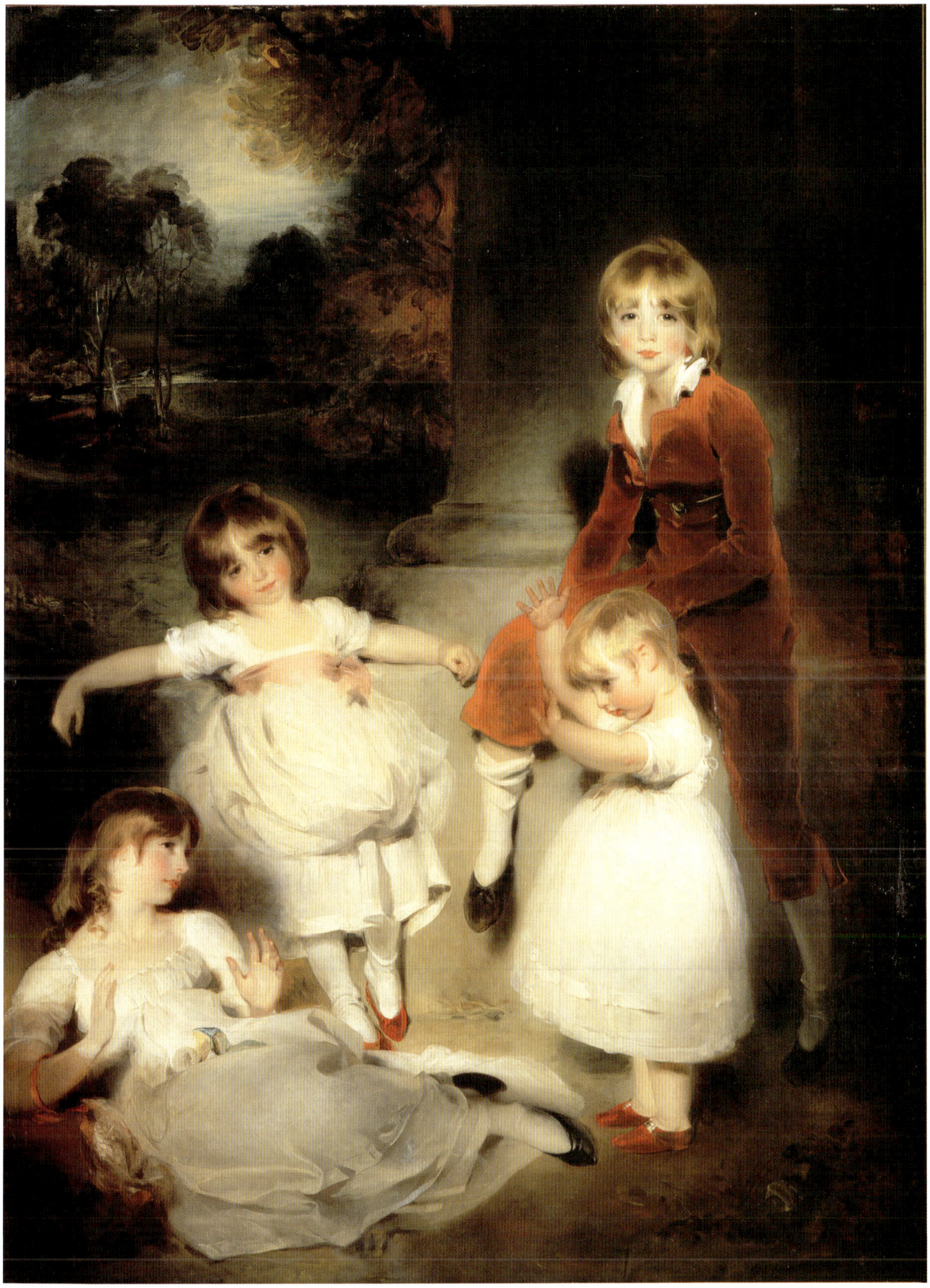

18 **Sarah Martha (Sally) Siddons** (1775-1803)
c. 1800
Pushkin Museum, Moscow, Russia.

Sally was the eldest daughter of Sarah and William Siddons. Lawrence was involved with Sally, with disastrous consequences. They were supposedly engaged when he turned his attentions briefly to her younger sister Maria. Realising his error, perhaps, he then returned his affections to Sally. Consumptive like her sister, Maria died in 1798. She is said, however, to have made Sally promise never to marry Lawrence. A number of drawings by Lawrence are said to represent Sally Siddons. Some are closer to stereotypes than portraits but, judging from those likely to be the most realistic, she seems to have borne a marked resemblance to her mother – though her face is somewhat softer – as shown in Lawrence's early portraits of her. Celilia Siddons, Mrs Siddon's youngest daughter, denied that either of her sisters ever sat for an oil portrait for Lawrence. Nevertheless, it is claimed that the portrait opposite represents Sally.

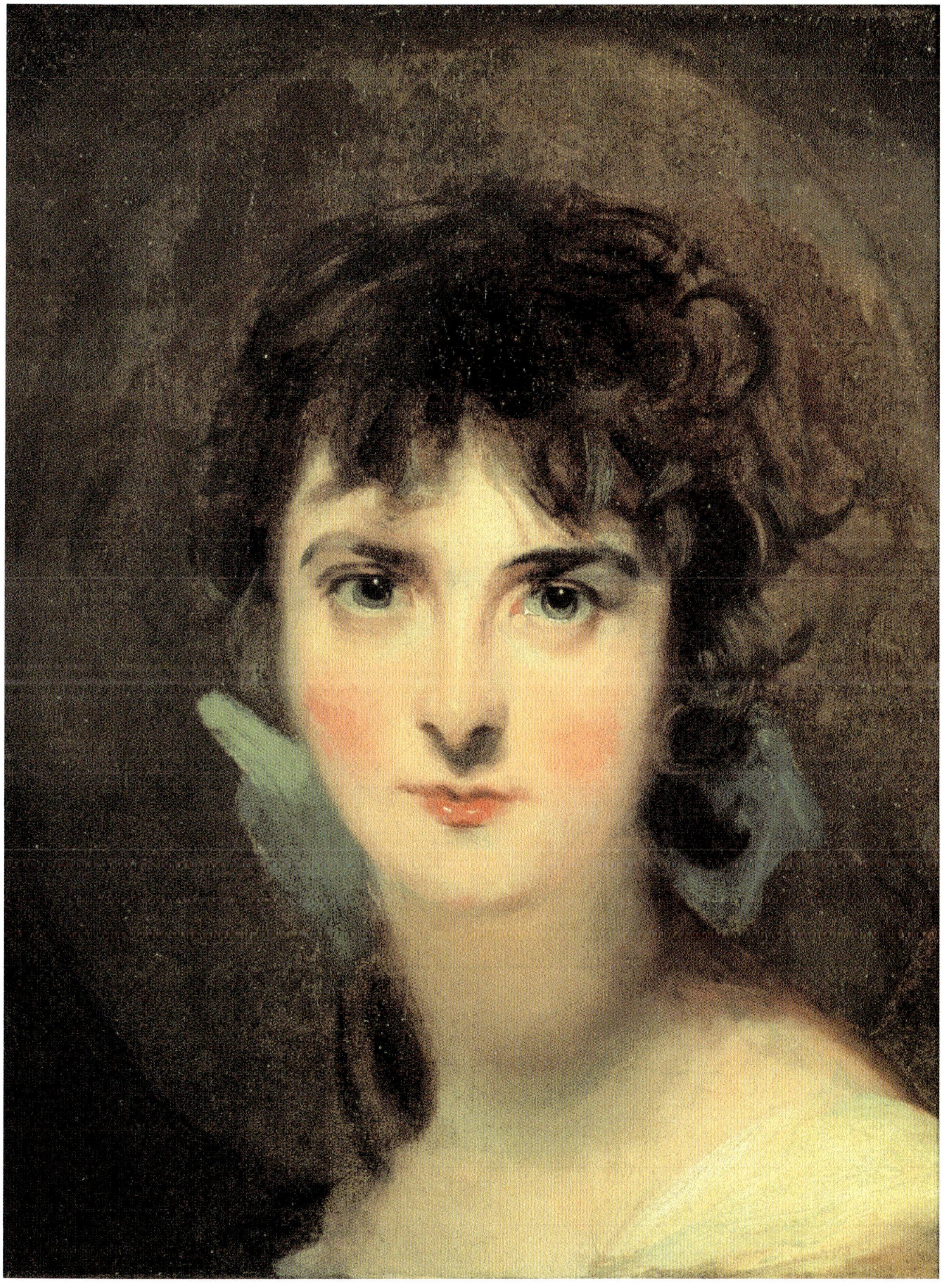

19 **The Hon. Charles James Fox, MP** (1749-1806)
Canvas $29\frac{3}{4}$ x $26\frac{1}{2}$ in. *c.* 1800
Private Collection

The third son of the 1st Baron Holland, Fox was a Whig statesman and opponent of Pitt the Younger. He held office only briefly as Britain's very first Foreign Secretary, in 1782, and assumed the role again in 1806. He also held office for a short time, under the Conservatives, as Joint-Secretary of State with Lord North under the Duke of Portland in 1783. Famously a champion of liberty and known as the 'Man of the People', he was a supporter of the revolutionary cause in France. Fearing as a youth that his 'natural idleness' would 'get the better of what little ambition I have', he clearly transcended his instincts.

Undertaking a long and ingenious vendetta against King George III, he remained for the most part in political opposition. As reckless in politics as at the gaming table, where it is thought that he lost the quite incredible sum of a quarter of a million pounds, his career was dogged by his wild – yet courageous – behaviour. When however in later life friends came to his financial rescue, he quit the gambling life for good, perhaps as a gesture of gratitude.

Strangely, given the fact that he was corpulent and lacking in elegance, he cut a dapper figure on the London scene. A fashion leader, he copied from the French court the most fashionable trends – extravagant laces and brocades, cosmetics and red heels – and brought them to London where they became *de rigueur*. The clear leader of that eminently fashionable group of men known as 'the Macaroni's', his sartorial know-how is not emphasized in Lawrence's portrait. His company was certainly sought after, particularly by the Duchess of Devonshire, who nicknamed him 'The Eyebrow' on account of his memorable brow.

Farington notes that Lawrence painted the portrait of Fox at St. Anne's Hill. The picture was handed down to Lord Holland, who did not hold it in great esteem, describing it as 'the worst ever painted of so eminent a man by so eminent an artist'.

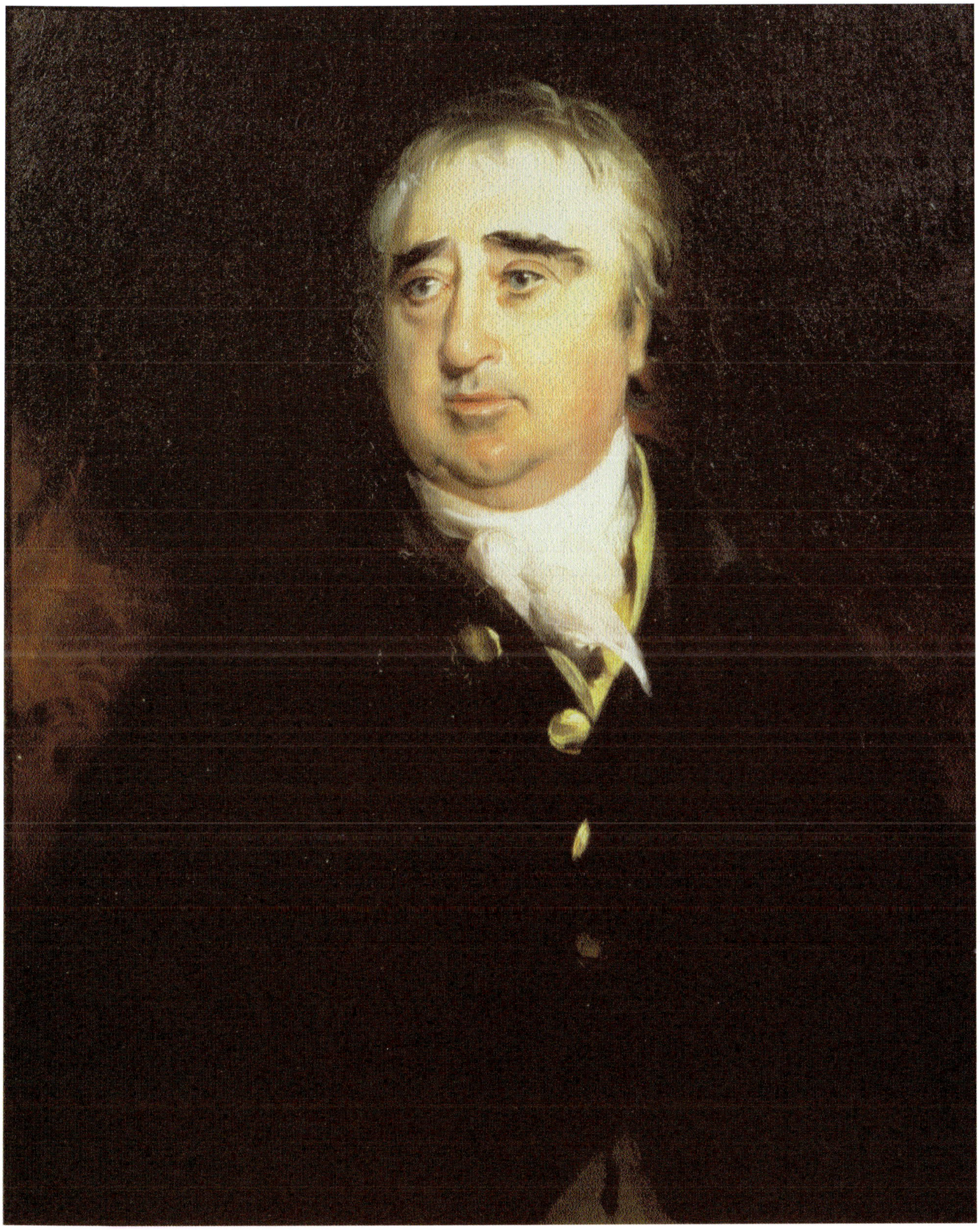

20 **John Philip Kemble as Hamlet**
Canvas 120 x 78 in. RA 1801 (187)
Tate Britain, London.

Kemble's first appearance in London was as Hamlet on 30 September 1783 at Drury Lane. In a letter of 1801 to Mrs. Boucherett, Lawrence refers to this picture in distinctly Hamletesque hyperbole.

'...I am very glad that, after the Two Friends, you like my Hamlet, which, except my Satan, I think my best work. I must try though, to give a something much better (for the low centre of your pier); for I begin to be really uneasy at finding myself so harnessed and shackled into this dry mill-horse business, which yet I must get through with steady industry, well knowing that this is the very season of my life when it is most necessary.

'How good you are to tell me of those friends who become dearer to me every hour in my life, and, I think, in exact proportion as I begin to see the real blessings of existence, and to prize what is valuable as I ought; only I have been a dreamer, and wake too late. I have lived half of my life; and though Death may not divide me from the being that I love, Circumstance (a creature of some potency) may as effectually do it, with more bitterness, if not equal sorrow. I am not fanciful enough to expect it otherwise'.

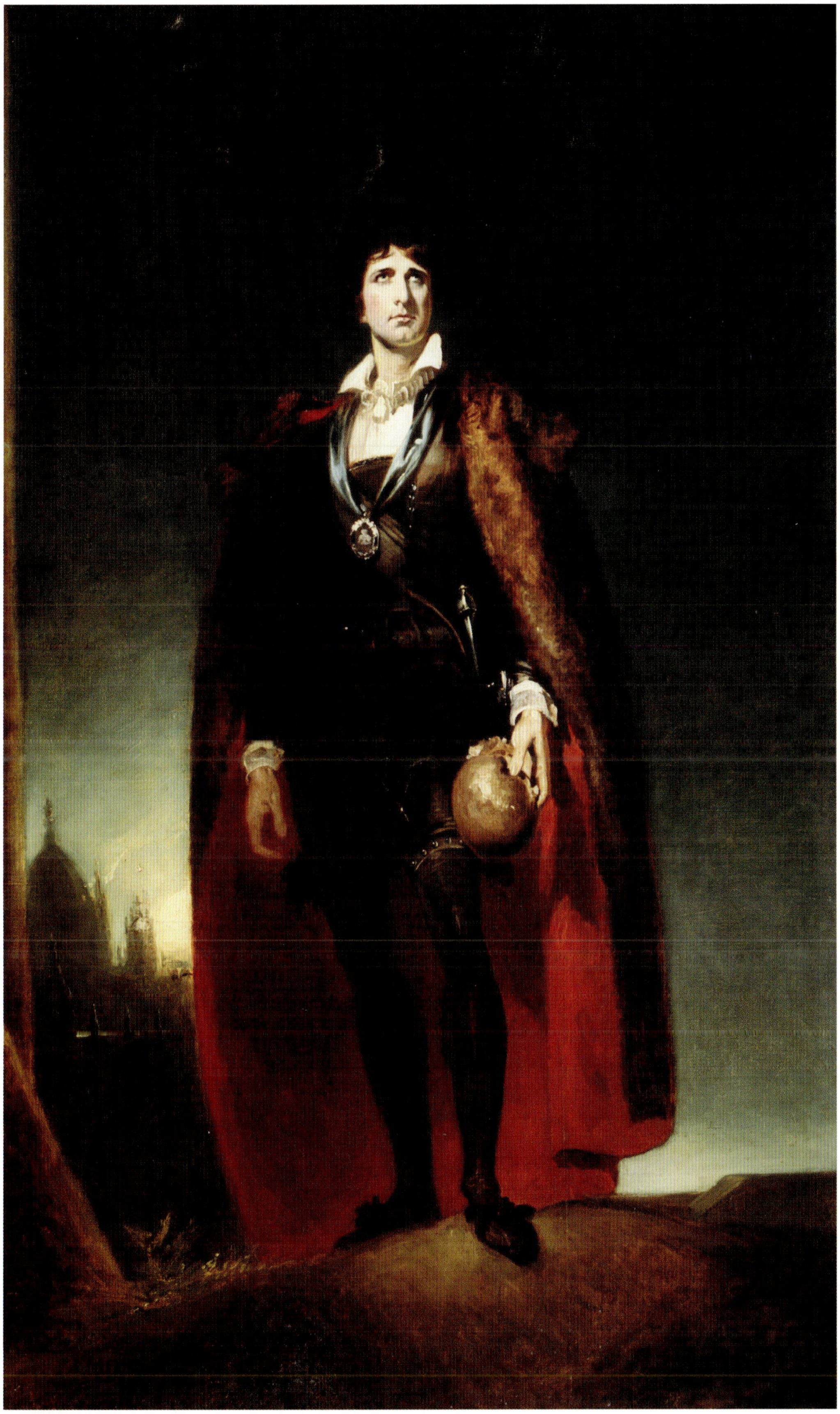

21 **Caroline, Princess of Wales (1768-1821) and Princess Charlotte (1796-1817)**
Canvas 119 x 81 in. 1801-02
RA 1802 (72)
H.M. the Queen, Buckingham Palace.

The 'Delicate Investigation' of 1806 threw suspicion on Lawrence's conduct whilst he was working on this picture. He denied any impropriety and Princess Caroline did the same.

'...He began a large picture of me and of my daughter, towards the latter end of the year 1800, or the beginning of 1801. Miss Garth and Miss Hayman were in the house with me at the time. The picture was painted at Montague House. Mr. Lawrence mentioned to Miss Hayman his wish to be permitted to remain some few nights in the house, that, by early rising, he might begin painting on the picture before the Princess Charlotte...or myself came to sit...At that time, Mr. Lawrence did not dine with me; his dinner was served in his own room. After dinner, he came down to the room where I and my ladies generally sat in an evening. Sometimes there was music, in which he joined, and sometimes he read poetry. Parts of Shakespeare's plays I particularly remember, from his reading them very well; and sometimes he played chess with me...he stayed in my house two or three nights together, but how many nights, in the whole, I do not recollect. The picture left my house in April 1801, and Mr. Lawrence never slept at my house afterwards.'

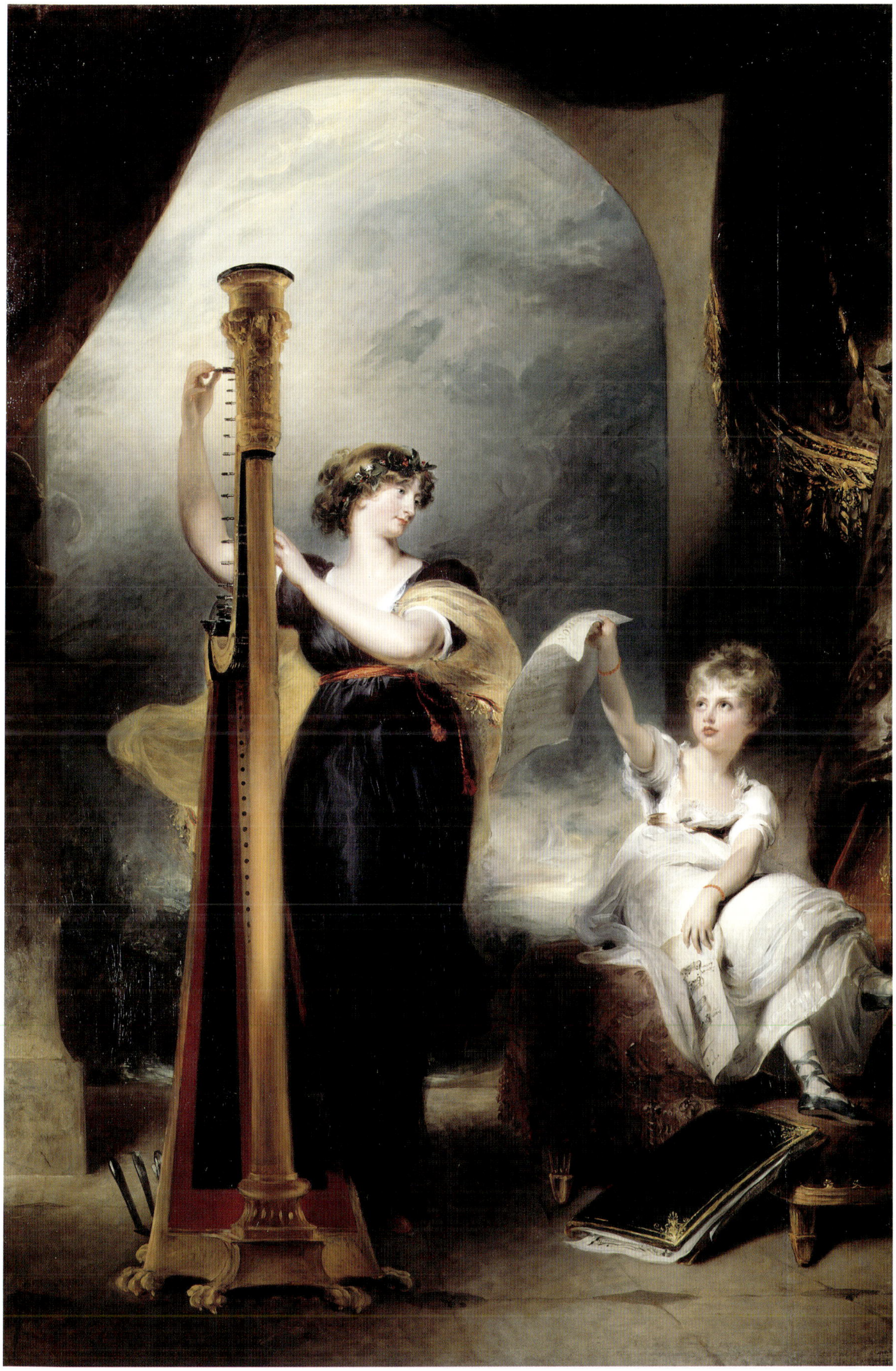

22 **The Hon. William Lamb, MP (later Lord Melbourne)** (1779-1848)
Canvas 30 x 25 in. *c.* 1805
Private collection.

Born in London to an aristocratic Whig family, William Lamb was the second son of the 1st Viscount Melbourne whom he succeeded in 1829. He was educated at Eton and Cambridge University where he met the Romantic Radicals Percy Bysshe Shelley, Lord Byron and their circle – in the long run perhaps to his detriment.

His early years were overshadowed by his disastrous and fateful marriage to Lady Caroline Ponsonby, (more usually known as Lady Caroline Lamb) who had a brief but very public affair with Byron, whom she continued to pursue for many years. The affair proved irresistable to the British gossip columns. Though he and his wife separated in 1825, her death three years later still came as an enormous blow.

He was Home Secretary from 1830-34 and Prime Minister from 1835-41 His influence on the young Queen Victoria was paramount. She had only just turned eighteen when she came to the throne in 1837 and over the next four years he advised her in the intricacies of politics. The two were so close that rumours even spread that they might marry. Yet Victoria, forty years his junior, whose father had died when she was a baby, clearly saw him as a father figure rather than potential husband.

Melbourne left a noteworthy body of reforming legislation. Among these were a reduction in the number of capital offences and reform of the Poor Laws and of local government. The city of Melbourne, Australia, was, in 1837, named in his honour.

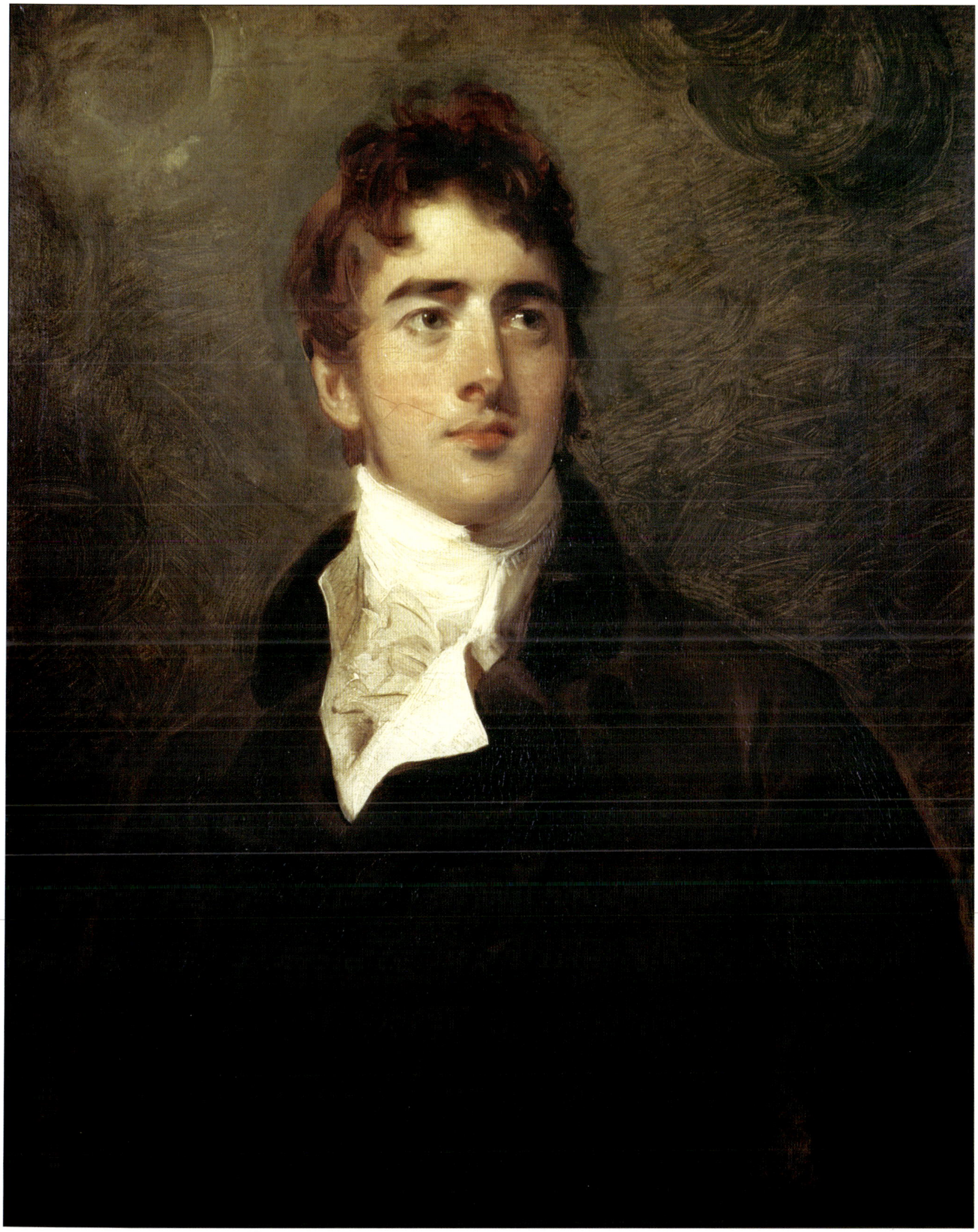

23 **Sir Francis Baring, 1st. Bart. (1740-1810), John Baring (1730-1816) and Charles Wall**

Canvas 61½ x 89 in. Begun 1806

RA 1807 (210)

Lord Northbrook Collection

Commissioned and painted as a pendant to Reynolds' triple portrait of Francis Baring's political associates Lord Ashburton, Lord Lansdowne and Colonel Barré, Lawrence's group was described by a critic of the 1807 RA exhibition as 'a fine Venetian picture, possessing all the luxuriance and splendour of Paul Veronese'. A letter from Lawrence to Farington received on 9 December 1807 indicated that for Baring he was prepared to relax his usually strict rule of painting only in his studio. The picture he mentions was probably another group portrait showing two of Sir Francis' children, Sir Thomas Baring and Mrs. Charles Wall with their families. The painting was eventually shown at the Royal Academy in 1810.

'To account for my stay here I must inform you first that it is greatly Sir Francis's wish who is more and more interested about the Picture and thinks I paint it here better than I can do in London. This is not true but I cannot make him think that it is not. In the next place I have work'd more constantly upon it (indeed every day) and the best consequence resulting from it is that as a picture it is very considerably advanced and, in my present opinion, successfully. – My time therefore will not have been trifled away, since by a Picture produced much below my present price, I shall have gain'd at the full rate, of your last calculation of my Income: These two essential considerations, will I know, have their weight with you…'.

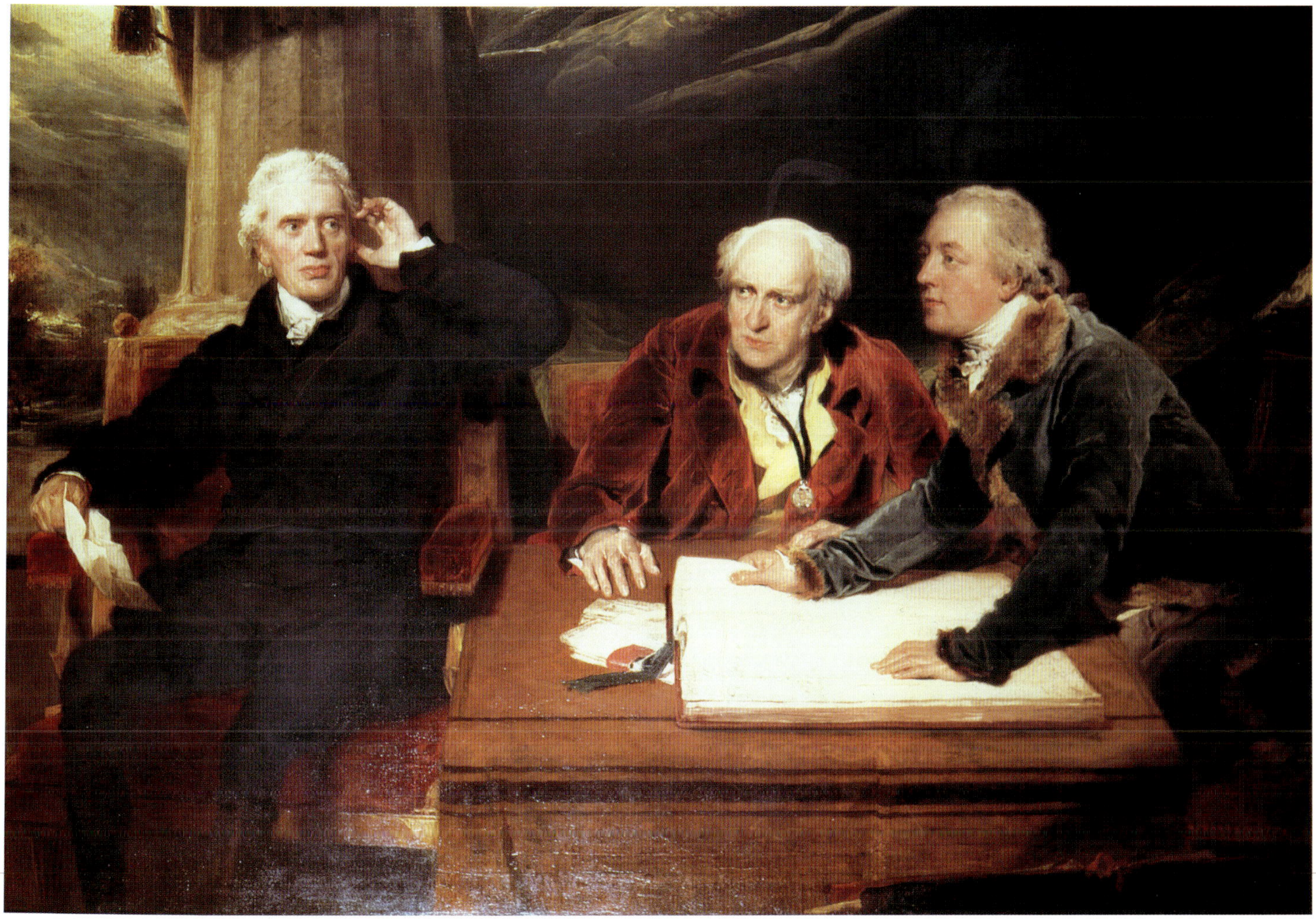

24 **Robert Stewart, Viscount Castlereagh, later 2nd Marquess of Londonderry** (1769-1822)
Canvas 29¼ x 24½ in.
RA 1810 (61)
National Portrait Gallery, London.

One of the most appealing and forthright of Lawrence's portraits of politicians, before he adopted the somewhat formal and theatrical poses of the 1820s, such as Sir Robert Peel and Lord Brougham.

Robert Stewart was the eldest surviving son of the 1st Marquess of Londonderry. He represented County Down in the Irish House of Commons in 1790 and after a busy political and military career in both Ireland and England, he was appointed Secretary for Ireland during the period preparatory to the Union with Britain. He was mostly concerned with Foreign Affairs after 1802 and was Secretary for War from 1805. He became Foreign Secretary in 1812 and organised the defeat of Napoleon. He succeeded his father as 2nd Marquess of Londonderry in 1821 but in 1822 committed suicide by cutting his throat with a penknife.

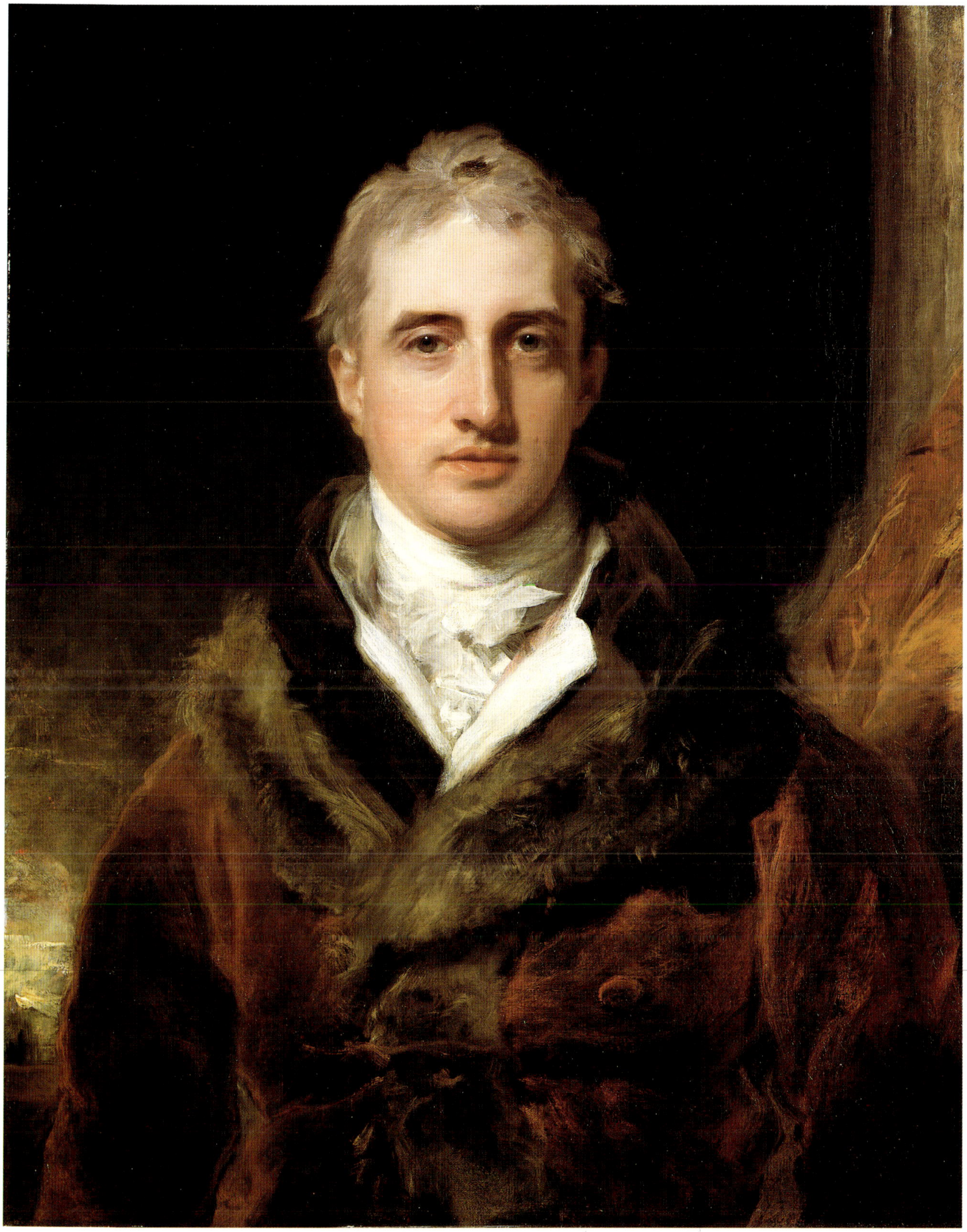

25 **Benjamin West, PRA** (1738-1820)
Panel 60 x 47½ in. 1810.
RA 1811 (113)
Yale Center for British Art, Paul Mellon Collection, New Haven, Connecticut.

A history and portrait painter from Pennsylvania, West spent most of his professional life in London and was a founder member of the Royal Academy, succeeding Reynolds as president in 1792. He was appointed historical painter to King George III in 1772. Notable for his influential transition to paintings featuring contemporary costume, his ideas have probably had more lasting impact than his actual work.

Looking somewhat stern, this three-quarter length portrait is the first of two that West sat for Lawrence.

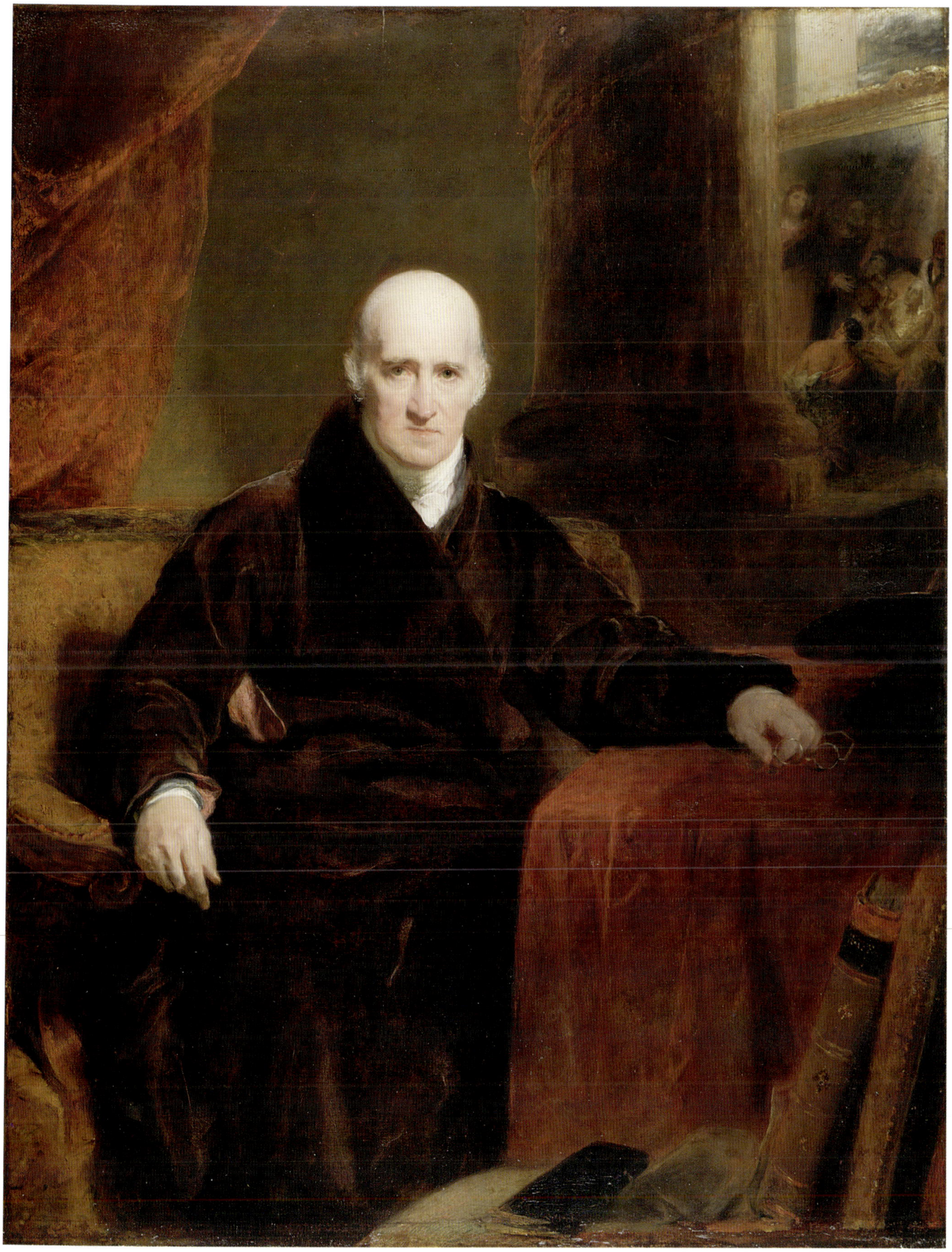

26 **Abu'l Hassan**
Canvas 35 x 27½ in. 1810
Fogg Art Museum, Harvard University Art Museums, Cambridge, Massachusetts

Abu'l Hassan, who died in 1846, was the Persian Ambassador, between 1809 and 1810, at the court of St. James. The portrait was commissioned by Sir Gore Ouseley while Abu'l Hassan was in London and taken with Sir Gore on his mission, as Ambassador Extraordinary, to conclude a treaty between the two countries.

A strange incident took place when the painting, temporarily placed on a sofa, was mistaken by the Persian Prime Minister. Mirza Shefi, who had never before seen a European oil painting, for the real person. He was said to have raged at the offending painting, 'I think that when the representative of the King of England does me the honour of standing up to receive me, in due respect to him, you should not be seated'. With the history of Persian painting so different to the western mimetic tradition, he said, 'I could have sworn by the Koran that it was a projecting substance – in truth, that it was Abu'l Hassan Khan himself'. Only when he had touched the painting had he realised his mistake.

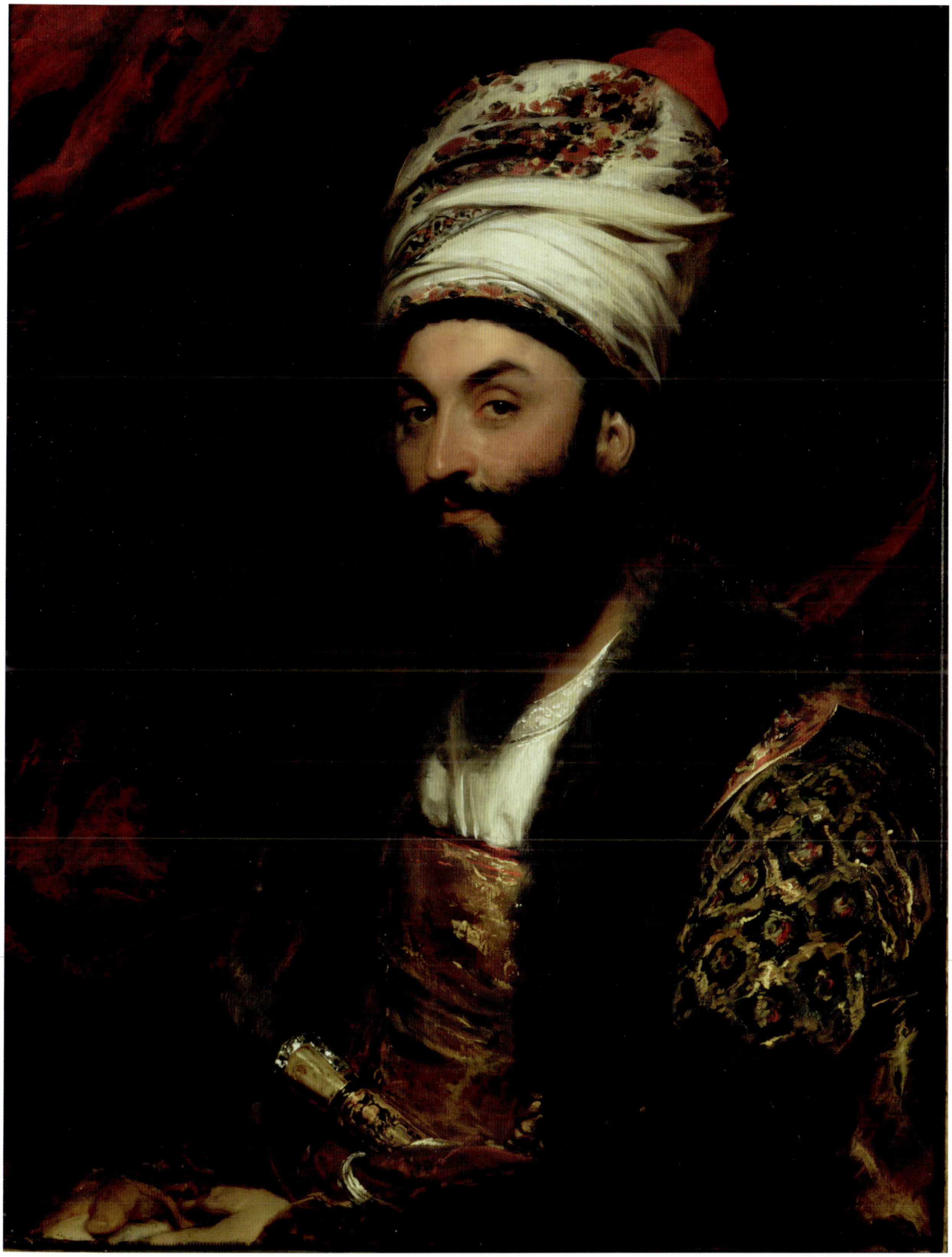

27 **Portrait of Arthur Wellesley, 1st Duke of Wellington** (1769-1852)
Canvas 36 x 28 in. *c.* 1815-16.
Apsley House, The Wellington Museum, London

This portrait, painted very shortly after Wellington's victory over Napoleon at Waterloo in 1815, convincingly expresses the stature of the sitter. In it Wellington is decorated with the Garter ribbon, the Star of the Garter and the Golden Fleece. As a character study Goya's portrait is often preferred; Lawrence here emphasises Wellington's confidence and control.

Wellington was born Arthur Wellesley, the third son of the 1st Earl of Mornington, in 1769 in Dublin. After an education at Eton and then military school, he entered the 73rd Infantry in 1787. His first active service was in the Netherlands campaign from 1793-4. In 1797 he was ordered to India where would defeat Tippoo Sahib. His service here was rewarded and he was entrusted to be the Governor of Mysore. Returning to England in 1805 he was in 1806 elected M.P. for the constituency of Rye in Sussex and shortly afterwards appointed Irish Secretary to the Duke of Portland. He did not leave the army behind however; in 1808 he was sent to Portugal where he conducted a successful campaign against the French, winning the battles of Talavera in 1809 and Salamanca in 1812 and finally Vimeiro, after which he returned home once again. However he was sent the following year to command the British in the Peninsular War; he drove the French from Spain and crowned his victory at Toulouse in 1814.

Among many other honours Wellesley was created the 1st Duke of Wellington. He was charged with defeating Napoleon – a victory for which we now remember him – and in return for which he was granted the estate of Strathfieldsaye. In 1818 Wellington reassumed his political career, joining the Tory government under Lord Liverpool. He finally became Prime Minister in 1828 but, standing firm in his refusal to amend the constitution in order to tackle an outbreak of angry riots in rural England in 1830, his popularity was severely diminished. In November that year the Government was defeated. He became Foreign Secretary under Peel; in 1846 he retired from politics altogether. Wellington died in 1852. He is buried in St. Pauls' Cathedral.

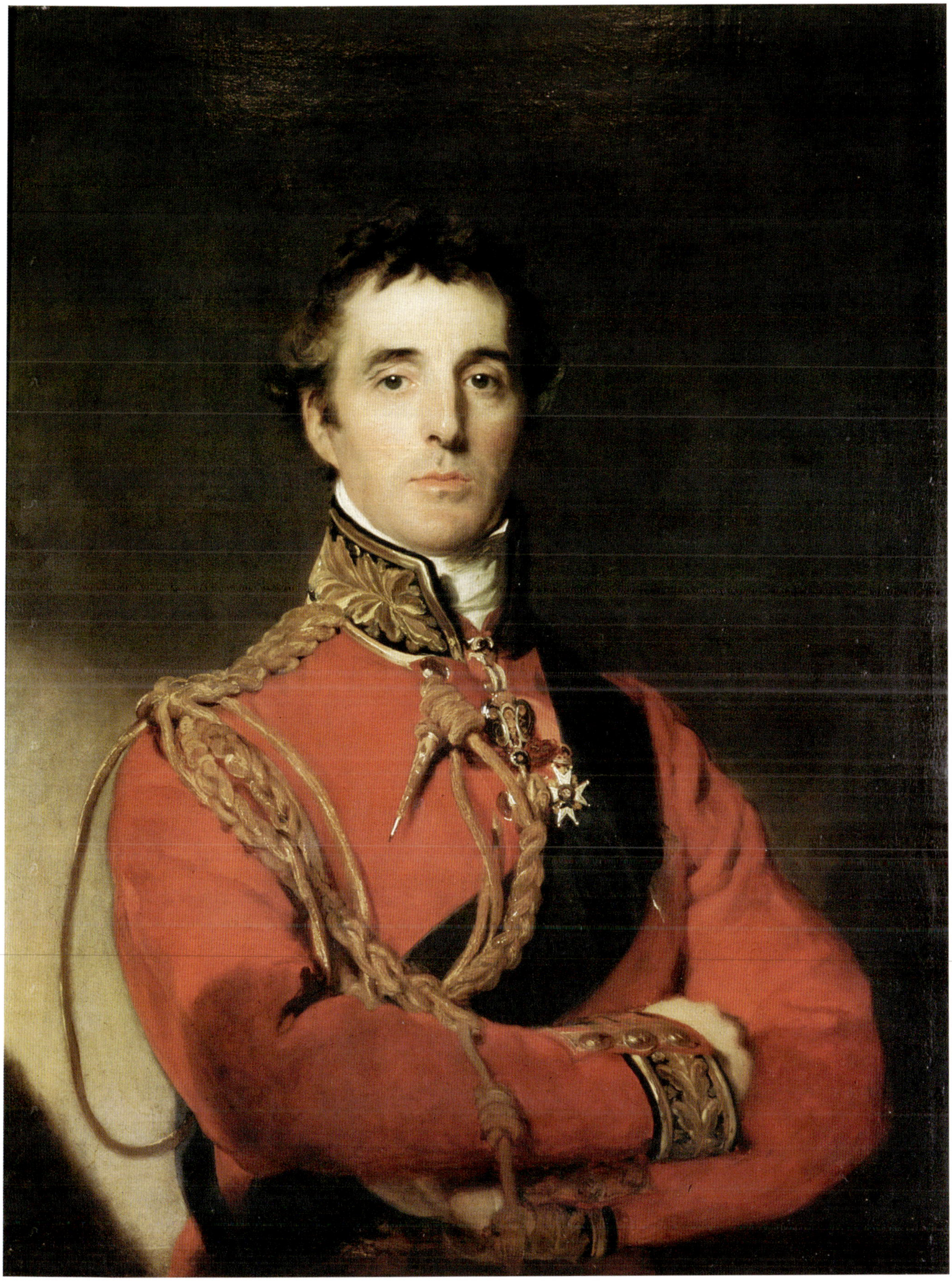

28 **Arthur Wellesley, 1st Duke of Wellington, KG, KB, MP** (1769-1852)
Canvas 124½ x 88¾ in. RA 1815 (109)
H.M. the Queen, Waterloo Chamber, Windsor Castle.

Painted to commemorate the Service of Thanksgiving for the first defeat of Napoleon. Wellington is shown in front of St. Paul's Cathedral, where the service took place, holding the Sword of State.

Lawrence's vast contribution to the 1815 RA, which included the large portraits of Platov, Blücher and the Prince Regent as well as this portrait and the smaller ones of Mrs. Wolff and Metternich, caused him considerable fatigue. He wrote to Farington, 'My professional exertions have been very unremitting since your departure from Town…I have painted more by Lamp Light than I have done for many Years, and many an Even'g have determin'd to close the employment of the Night by communication with you, when very weariness has rendered me unfit for the attempt…I am glad to tell you that I succeed in the completion of Lord Wellington's Portrait. From its very size and necessary accompaniments it has been a great Fag to me, and demanded more constancy of Labor, and vigilant attention than, I think, any Picture I have painted…'Tis hard to toil and struggle for some subtle refinement of a Tone or harmony of Lines that shall unite a whole, where the Parts have been of arduous execution, in order to meet the prompt decision of one rapid glance of Ignorance!…'
.

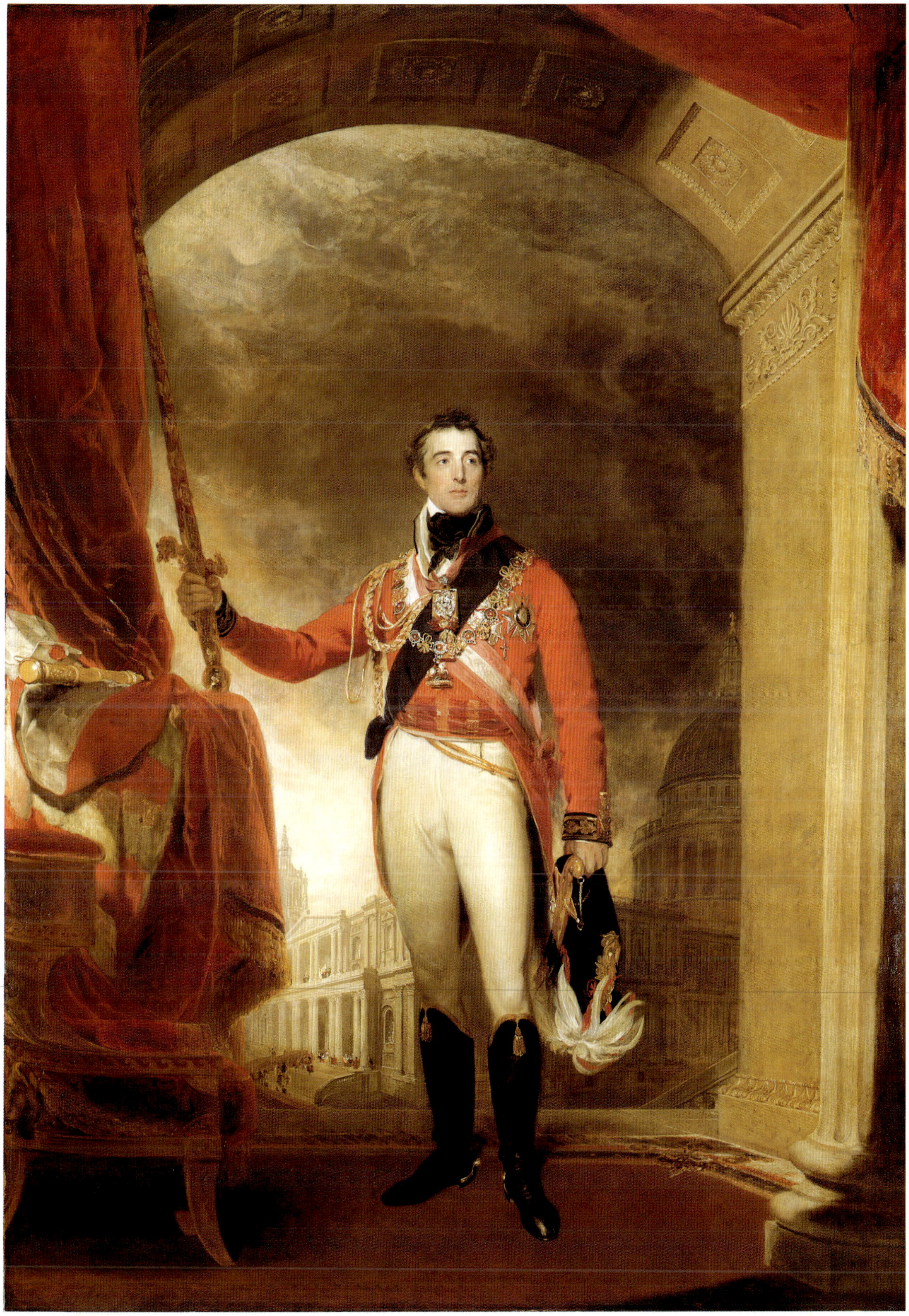

29 **Mrs. Jens Wolff** (1771-1829)
Canvas 50 x 40 in. RA 1815 (28)
Art Institute, Chicago.

Isabella Ann was the daughter of Norton Hutchinson of Woodhall Park. She married Jens Wolff, joint Danish Consul, London. But they separated in 1810. It was around this time that she had a son, Herman. She claimed that she and Jens had no children, and the suspicion is that Herman was in fact the son of her and Lawrence. Renforced by the intense interest shown in the child by Lawrence, who sketched him and once took him to Paris. Regardless, there is little doubt that Lawrence was clearly in love with Mrs Wolff, a good decade after the Siddons family debacle.

This portrait was commissioned by Mrs Clarissa Hill, Wolff's sister, in 1802 but was not completed until 1815. Unsurprisingly Clarissa was upset by the length of time that had passed. Wolff poses as the Eryhthraen Sibyl from the Sistine Chapel ceiling. She was studying a book of Michelangelo's engravings. The background details of a roman lamp and statue reflect Jens Wolff's interest in the antique. After her divorce she lived with her sister Cassandra Marshall in Kent where Lawrence was a regular visitor.

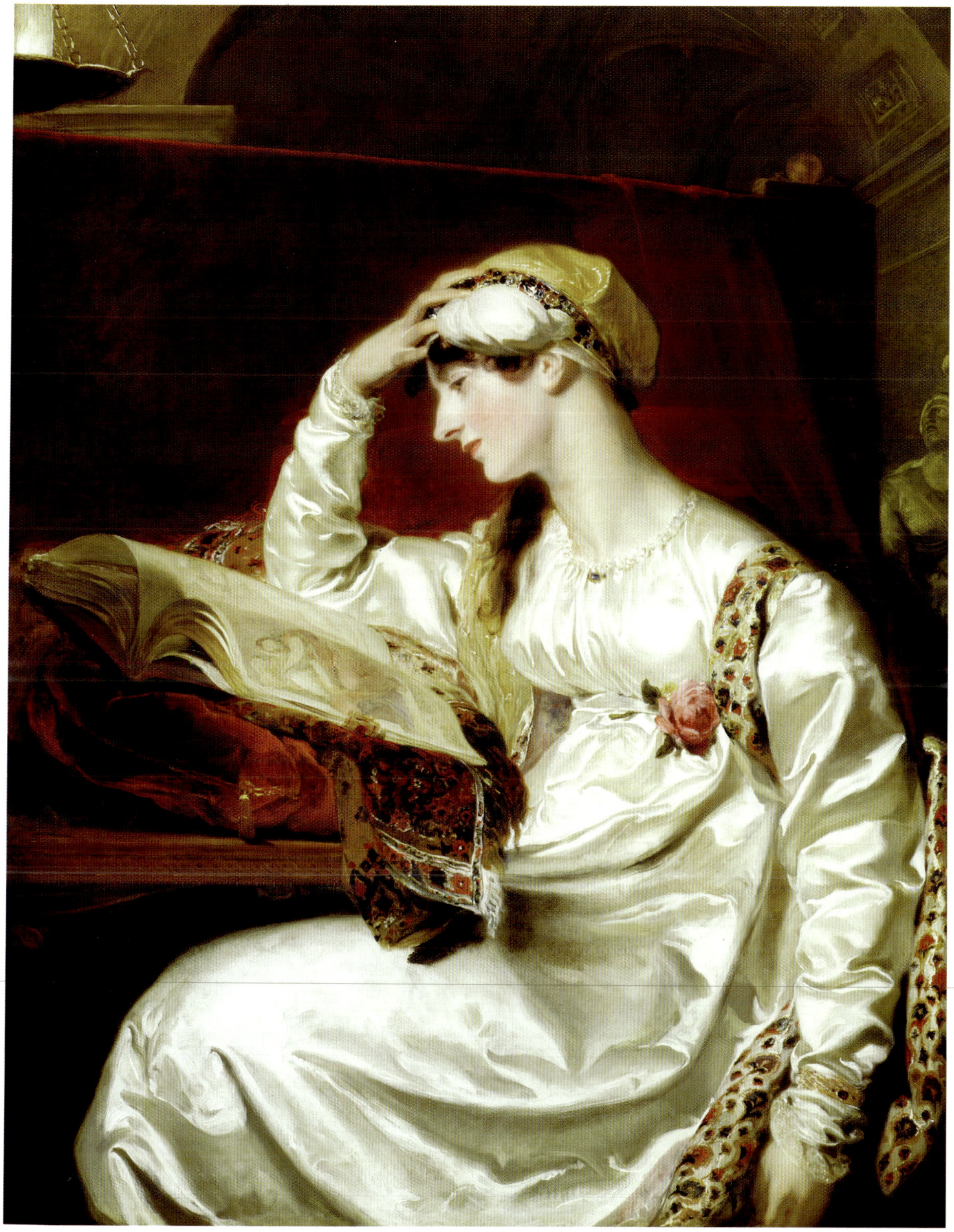

30 **Sir Humphry Davy** (1778-1829)
Canvas 56 x 52 in. 1815
Royal Institution, London.

Humphry Davy, a pioneer in the field of electro-chemistry, may not now be as well known as certain of his discoveries – most amusingly to contemporary society that of 'laughing gas'. Lawrence here paints a portrait of a kindly but confident figure.

Born in Penzance, Davy was apprenticed after his father's death to a surgeon-apothecary. He was later to become superintendant of the Medical Pneumatic Institution in Bristol, which was devoted to the study of various gases and their possible use in the medical field. It was through his important work in electro-chemistry that he met Michael Faraday, who worked as his assistant, and the two became firm friends and colleagues.

In 1801 he became a lecturer at the Royal Institution, in 1803 becoming a fellow of the Royal Society, and its president from 1820 to 1827. His reputation chiefly rests on his discovery that chemical compounds can be decomposed, using electricity, into their elements, and his subsequent discovery of potassium, sodium, barium, strontium, calcium, and magnesium. He was knighted in 1812 and toured Europe from 1813 to 1815 with his wife and then with Faraday. After returning to England, Davy was prolific in his discoveries and in knowing how best they might be used, inventing for example a miner's safety lamp as well as chemical approaches to agriculture and the tanning and mineralogy industries. He also invented a process that could be used to desalinate sea water and came up with the idea of attaching zinc plates to copper-clad ships as protection from the elements.

In 1827, Davy became seriously ill – his condition was thought to have been caused by the numerous gases he had inhaled throughout his career. He died in 1829.

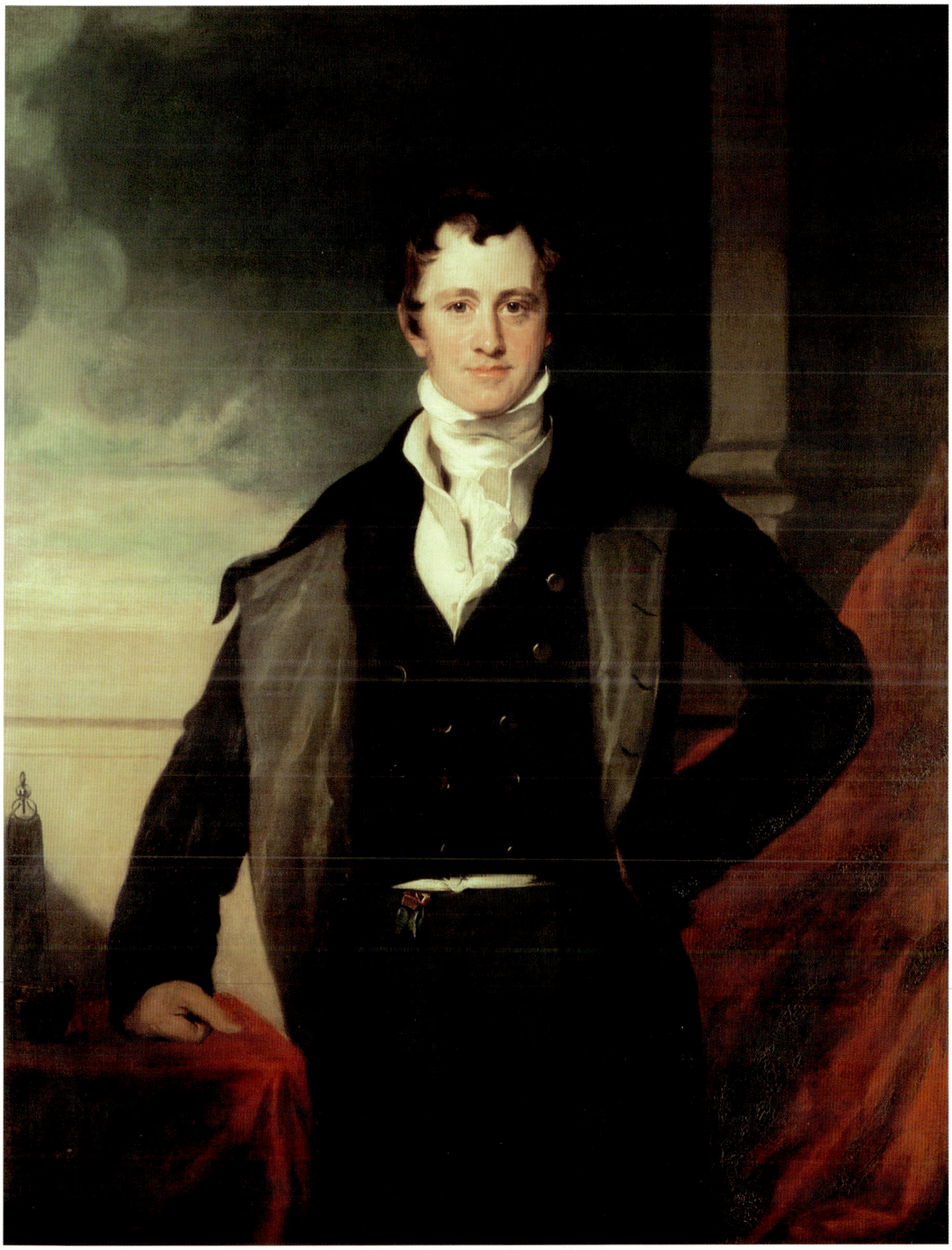

31 **Field-Marshal Gebhardt von Blücher** (1742-1819) Canvas $106\frac{1}{2}$ x $70\frac{1}{4}$ in. RA 1815 (155)
H.M. the Queen, Waterloo Chamber, Windsor Castle.

Lawrence's friend Miss Elizabeth Croft called on the artist whilst he was painting the Field-Marshal and described the visit in her Recollections of the artist:

'When he was painting the heroes Blücher and Platov, in 1814 all the town seem'd running mad to get a sight of them. A piece of good fortune befel me in consequence of my calling one day on Mrs. Bloxam in Russel Square. Holman opened the door to me and said Mrs. Bloxam was out, and Sir Thos. engaged with the "Field Marshal". I left my card and had proceeded only a few yards when Holman came running to say his master begg'd I would return. Sir Thomas came down to me looking harassed and distressed, and said, "They have sent Blücher to me without any attendant or interpreter. He has been travelling all night from Portsmouth and is evidently half-seas-over, and consequently falls asleep the moment I cease talking to him; and moreover, being somewhat deaf, I can only make him hear by going quite close to him"... Finding Blücher only spoke German and very bad French, I felt less afraid and was introduced...It was very convenient that he did not understand our English, as Sir Thomas prompted me as to the best means of keeping him awake...In the commencement of my office Sir Thos. imposed a difficult task on me, which was to request he would curl up his moustaches so that they might not cover his lower as well as upper lip – this with my bad French I found difficult to make him comprehend, but I at length accomplished it more by signs than words, and putting his filthy fingers into his mouth, he brought them out plentifully wet, and curled the moustaches into a smaller compass....The mob in Russel Square rushed in in a frightful manner even the first time Blücher sat, lining the staircase and filling the gallery; and at length it was scarcely possible to keep them out of the painting room, except by the aid of Bow Street officers'.

Blücher, proud of having risen from the ranks to command the army of Silesia, was Commander in Chief of the army of the Lower Rhine at Waterloo and made the decisive intervention in support of Wellington towards the end of the battle.

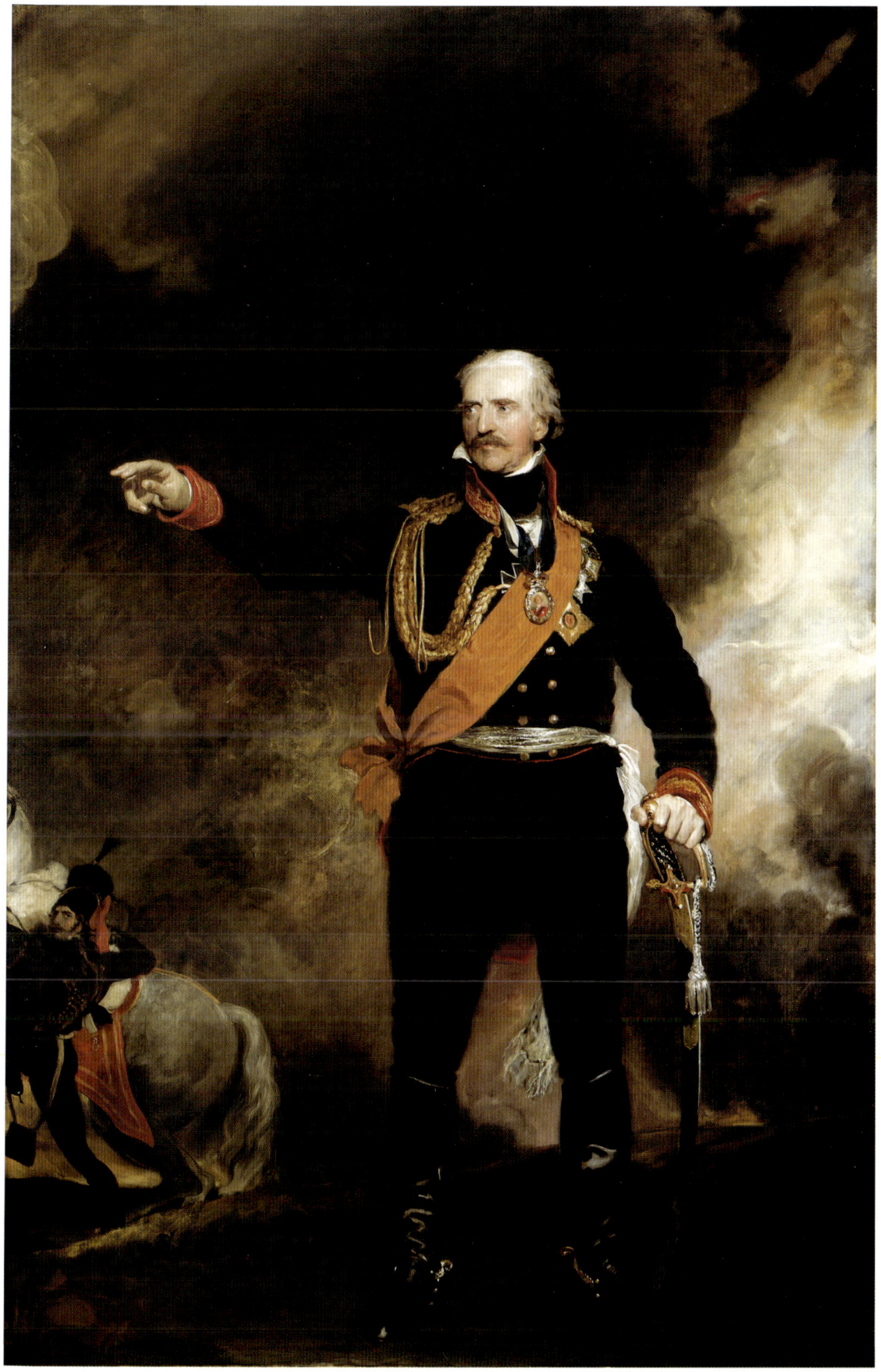

32 **Ivanovitch, Count Platov** (1757-1818)
Canvas 106 x 70½ in. RA 1815 (163)
H.M. the Queen, Waterloo Chamber, Windsor Castle.

One of the first portraits commissioned by the Prince Regent for the future Waterloo Chamber series. Platov wrote to Lawrence on 'Monday morning' in 1814 to announce his intention of sitting.

'His Excellency Count Platoff's Compt. to Mr. Lawrence is directed by Captn. Jackson to say he will wait on him tomorrow morning at 11 o' clock to sit for His Picture, according to the wish and desire of His Royal Highness The Prince Regent'.

Lawrence's studio was guarded by mounted Cossacks whilst Platov was inside. The portrait was a great success although a number of sketches sold at the posthumous sales and the extensive pentimenti suggest that it caused Lawrence some difficulty.

Platov commanded the Cossacks in their pursuit of the French away from Moscow to Paris.

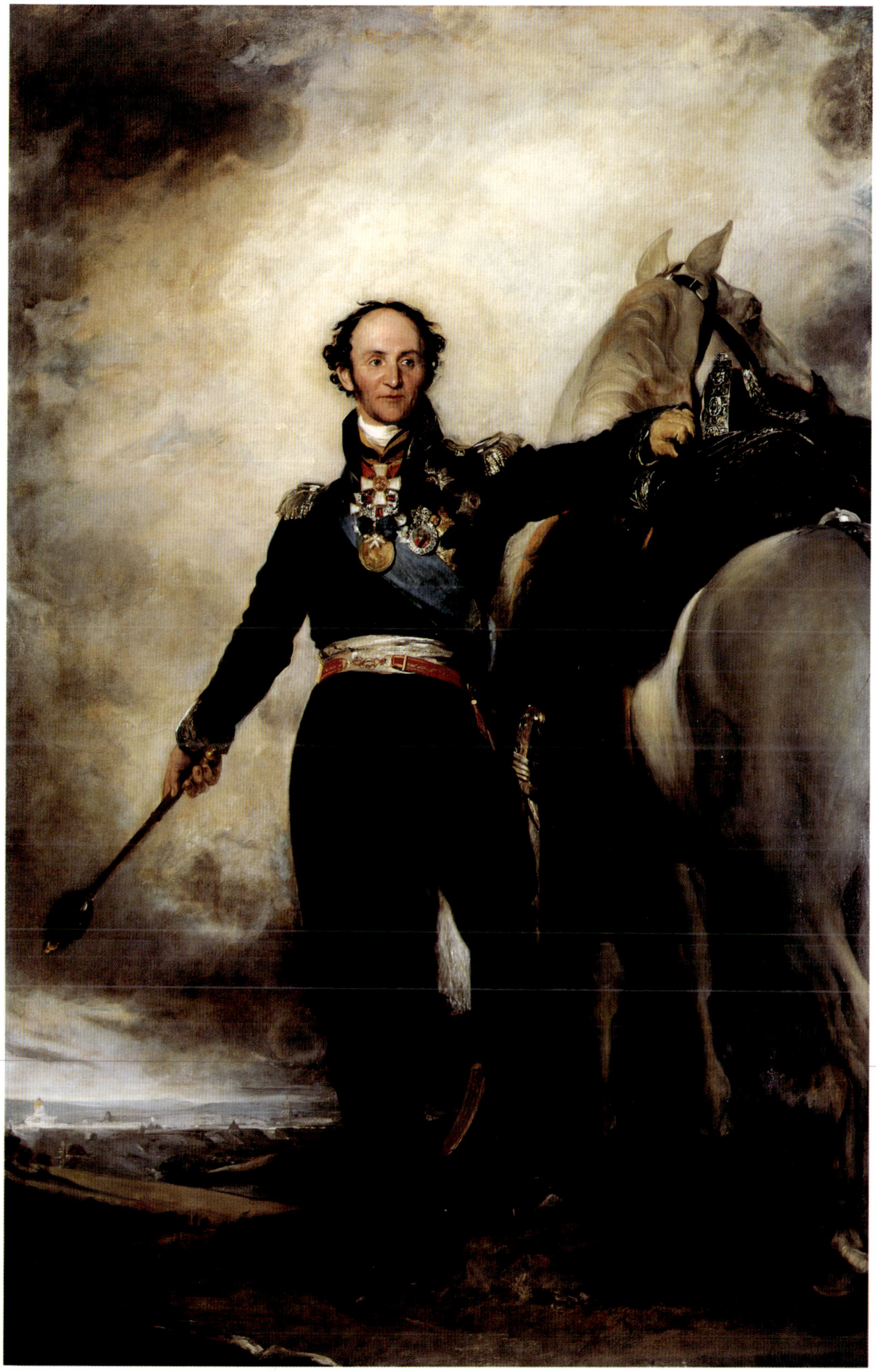

33 **Clemens Lothar Wenzel, Prince Metternich** (1773-1859)
Canvas 52½ x 41½ in. RA 1815 (76)
H.M. the Queen, Waterloo Chamber, Windsor Castle.

Lawrence mentions a version of this portrait in his letter to Elizabeth Croft, dated 10 January 1819, from Vienna.

'.....To-morrow I shall have the pleasure of improving my picture of Prince Metternich, which, though it is so universally liked, from the popularity of the original, and its being a close resemblance of him, is at present below the character of his countenance.....'

Lawrence seems to have been 'improving' his portrait of Metternich in Aix-la-Chapelle and Rome as well as Vienna. It was one of the portraits that he carried with him, like those of Platov and Blücher, as an example of his work. He painted several replicas.

Metternich was Austrian Minister in Dresden, Berlin and then Paris during the Napoleonic wars. From 1809 to 1848 he was the Austrian Foreign Minister, attempting to retain a state of peaceful equilibrium between the European powers.

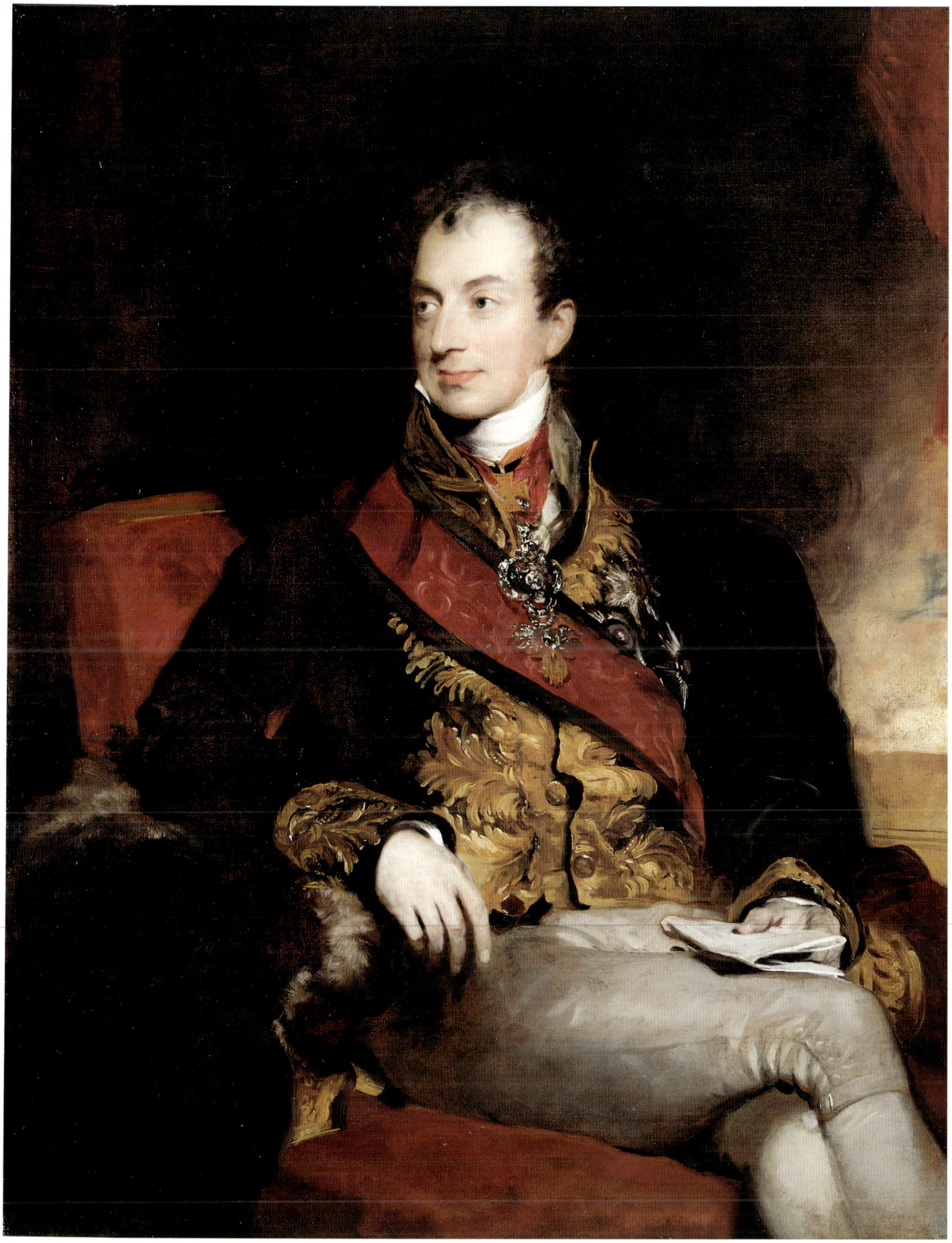

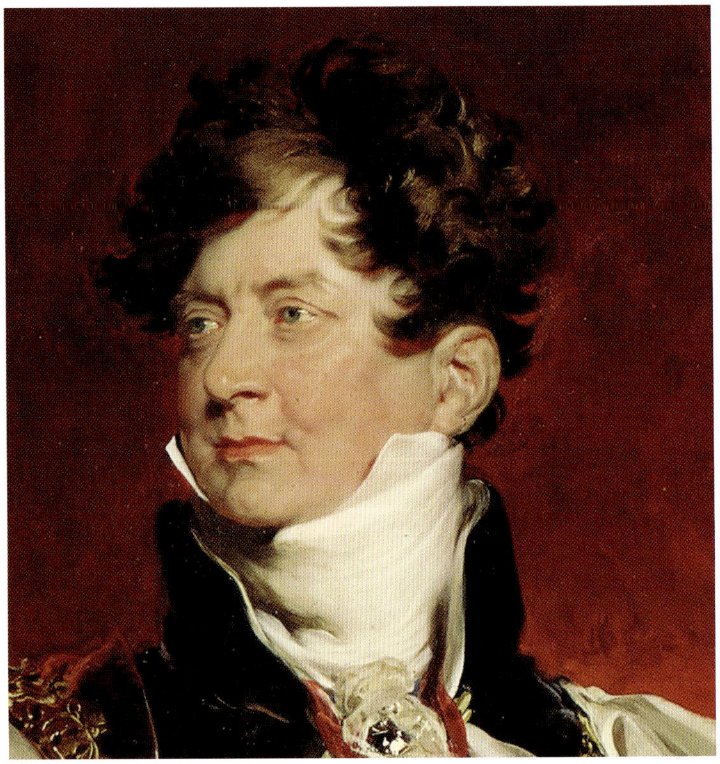

34 **George IV** (1762-1830)
Canvas 115 x 80 in. 1816
Vatican Museums and Galleries, Vatican City, Italy

Lawrence's first portrait of George IV, commissioned by Lord Charles Stewart. In July 1814 he wrote to Lawrence announcing the Prince Regent's decision to sit.

'The Prince has fix'd tomorrow about 2 o' clock for me to accompany him to see the portraits [of Blücher and Platov] and perhaps to sit – He may however disappoint, but you had best be prepared'.

The Prince was thrilled with Lawrence's picture which, as Hazlitt commented in *The Champion*, was a ridiculously flattering image.

'Sir Thomas Lawrence has with the magic of his pencil recreated the Prince Regent as a well-fleshed Adonis of thirty-three; and, happy as we always are to contemplate the innocent happiness of others, even when it is not referable to the most philosophic sources of human satisfaction, we could not, as we stood before this very admirable picture but derive a high degree of goodnatured pleasure from imagining to ourselves the transports with which his Royal Highness must have welcomed this improved version of himself. It goes far beyond all that wigs, powders, and pomatums have been able to effect for the last twenty years'.

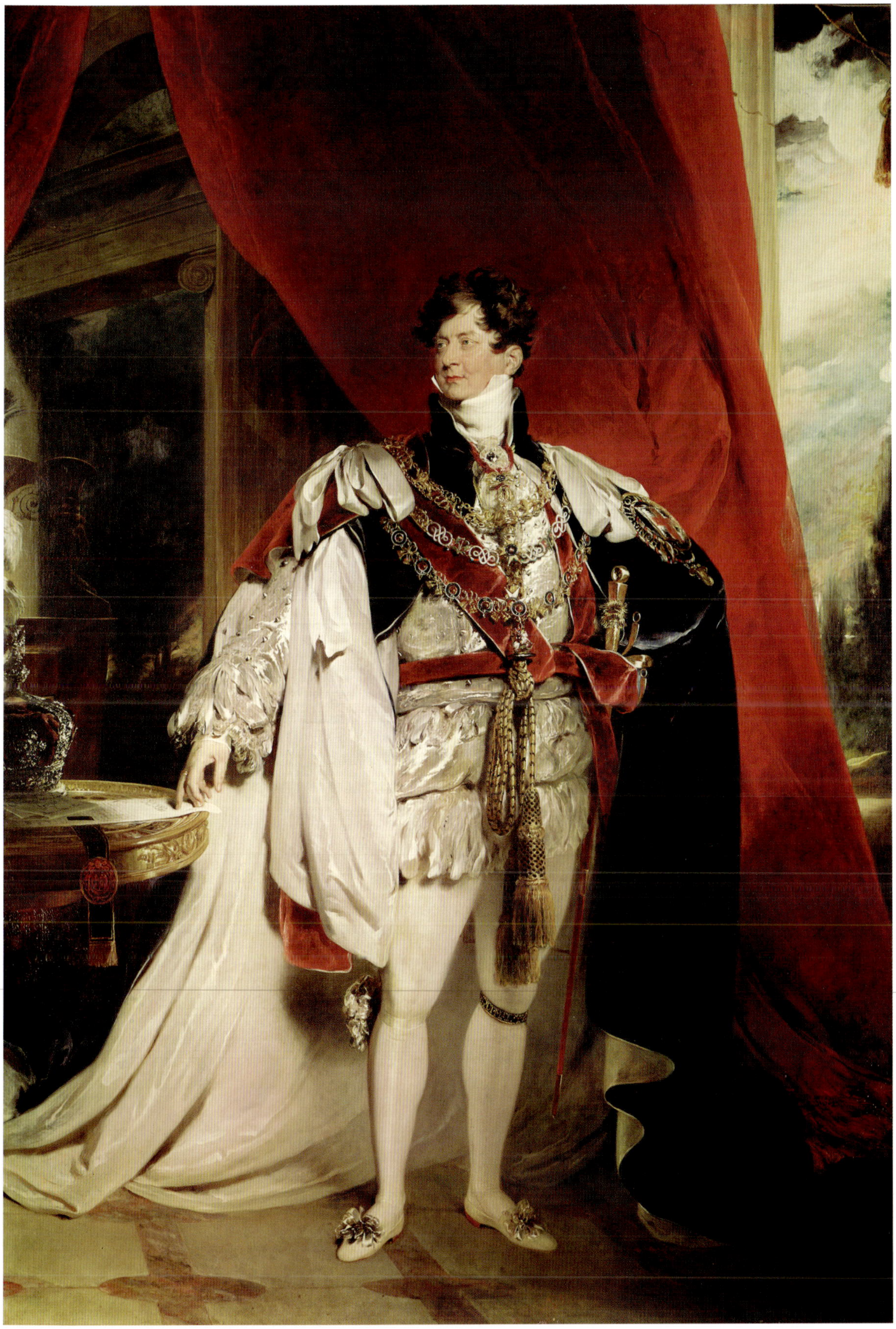

35 **Antonio Canova** (1757-1822)
Canvas 35½ x 28 in. 1816
Museo Civico, Treviso, Italy

The most successful and important of the Neo-classical sculptors, Antonio Canova was born in Possagno, near Treviso, and he moved to Venice in 1768. His origins as a stonemason are to be found in his emphasis on personal handling of his work, even when running a large studio. His later work, after his move to Rome in 1781, owed a huge debt to Antiquity. Canova worked for such eminents as Napoleon and the Duke of Wellington. On behalf of the Pope, who, in 1816 created him Marchese d'Ischia for his troubles, he was instrumental in securing the return to the papacy of the works of art taken to France by Napoleon.

Lawrence painted his picture – at least twenty versions are known, some only showing the head – when in November 1816 he came to England. Here the sculptor examined the Elgin marbles, despite turning down Lord Elgin's earlier request to restore them because 'it would be sacrilege in him or any man to presume to touch them with a chisel.' Lawrence and Canova struck up a firm friendship, which they maintained by letter, undoubtedly fuelled in part by their shared reverence for the work of the Ancients.

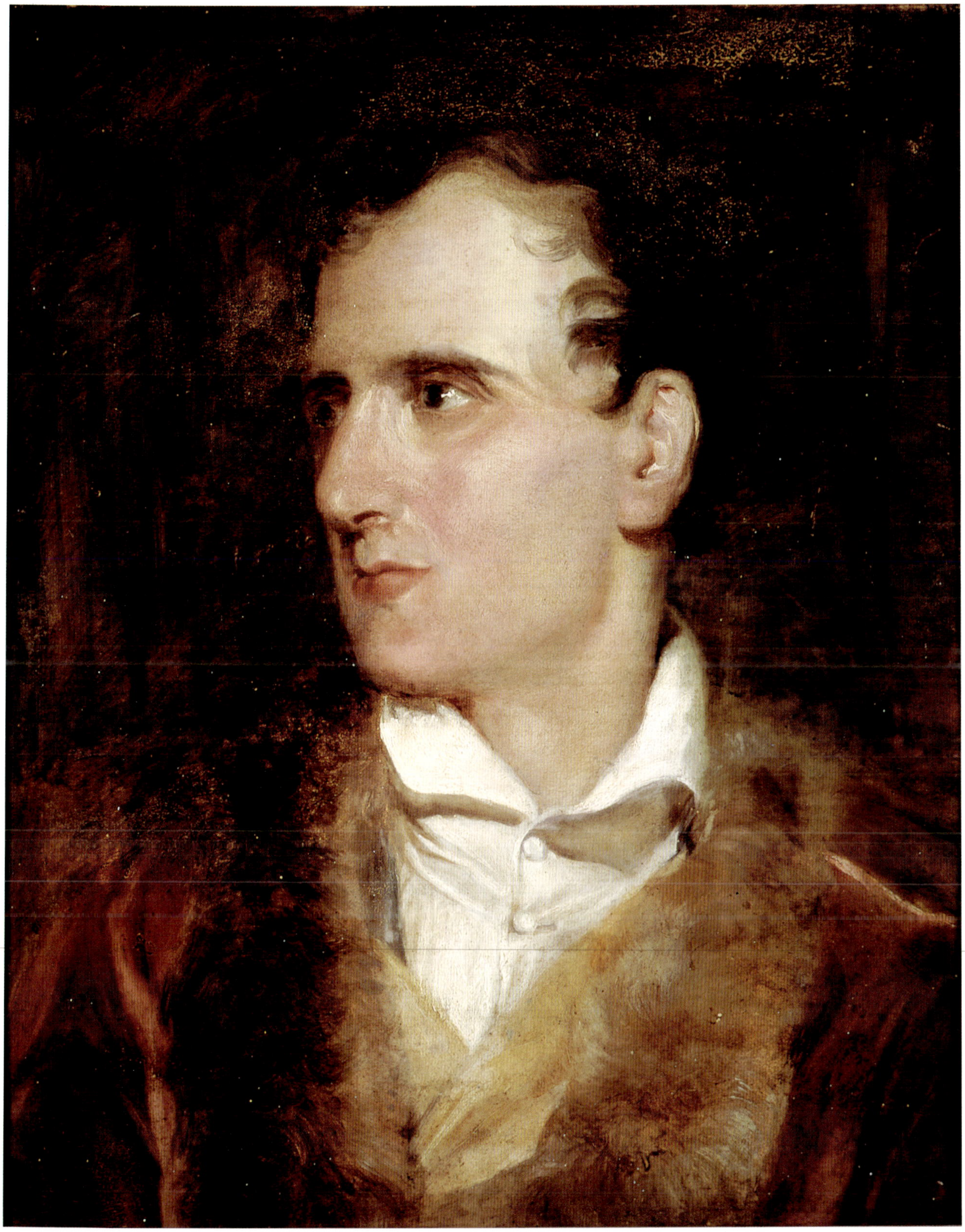

36 **Alexander I, Emperor of Russia** (1777-1825)
Canvas 107½ x 70½ in. 1814-18
H.M. the Queen, Waterloo Chamber, Windsor Castle.

Commenced in London in 1814 and completed in Aix-la-Chapelle with seven sittings in 1818. The Emperor's rather peculiar pose was a successful reproduction of reality. Lawrence described the difficulty of capturing it accurately in a letter to Mrs. Wolff.

'I had…to make a total alteration in the picture, changing entirely the action of the legs, and consequently of the trunk. You will readily imagine that, circumstanced as I am, I work with the utmost vigilance of eye, – I never exerted this with more certain effect than in drawing in that very action. The process was new to the Emperor, and the accuracy with which it was done surprised and pleased him. All seeing in it an unusual action of his Majesty, gave it their unanimous approbation, and I, only on the day after saw its defect, and at all hazards determined to amend it.

'He stands always resting on one leg – (you know what I mean, the other loose on the ground, like the figures of the antique) – and he stands either with his hat in his hand or with his hands closely knit before him. The first figure was thus [pen and ink thumbnail sketch of Emperor]. You perceive that he here seems to be shrinking and retiring from the object of his contemplation, determining at the same time to preserve and hold fast one certain good from the enemy, whatever may be the issue of the battle. These were my objections, and the vexatious thing was, that, before an audience of his friends, I was to commence the alteration, by giving him four legs, and though gradually obliterating the two first; still their agreeable lines were remaining in most complicated confusion. What I expected took place; during almost the whole of it, the attendant generals complained, and the Emperor, though confiding in my opinion, was still dissatisfied. However, I accomplished the alteration and the vessel righted'.

Alexander succeeded his father, Paul I, in 1801.

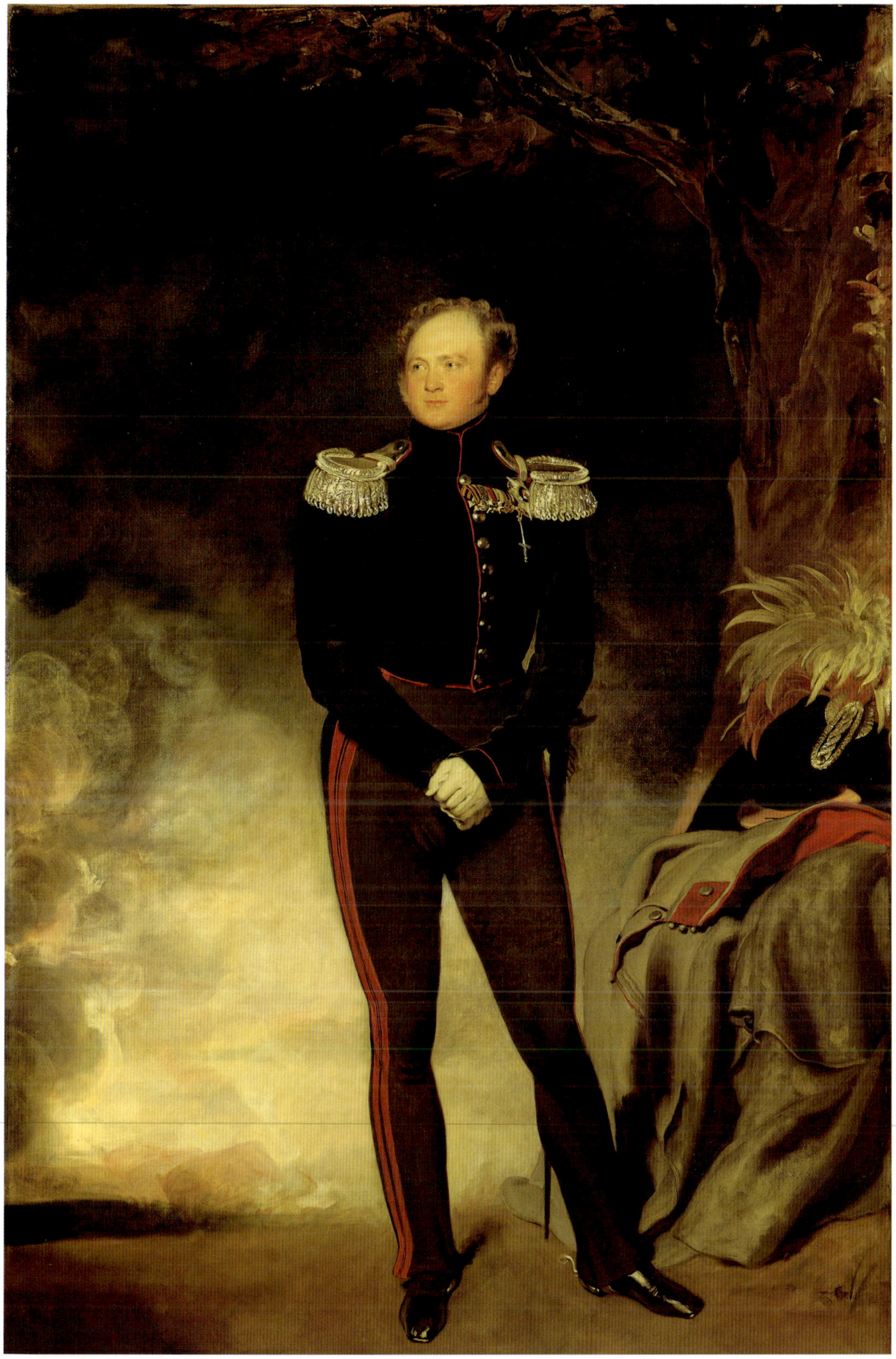

37 **Frederick William III, King of Prussia**
(1770-1840)
Canvas $106\frac{1}{2}$ x $70\frac{1}{4}$ in. 1814-18
H.M. the Queen, Waterloo Chamber, Windsor Castle.

This portrait was begun in London in 1814 and finished in Aix-la-Chapelle, where the king gave Lawrence six sittings, in 1818. Lawrence wrote from Aix on 26 November to his niece, Lucy Ann Bloxam: '...the King of Prussia is taller than either [the Emperors of Russia and Austria] but with more reserve of manner. He has good features and is of a sincere and generous nature...'.

Frederick William III succeeded his father, Frederick William II, in 1797.

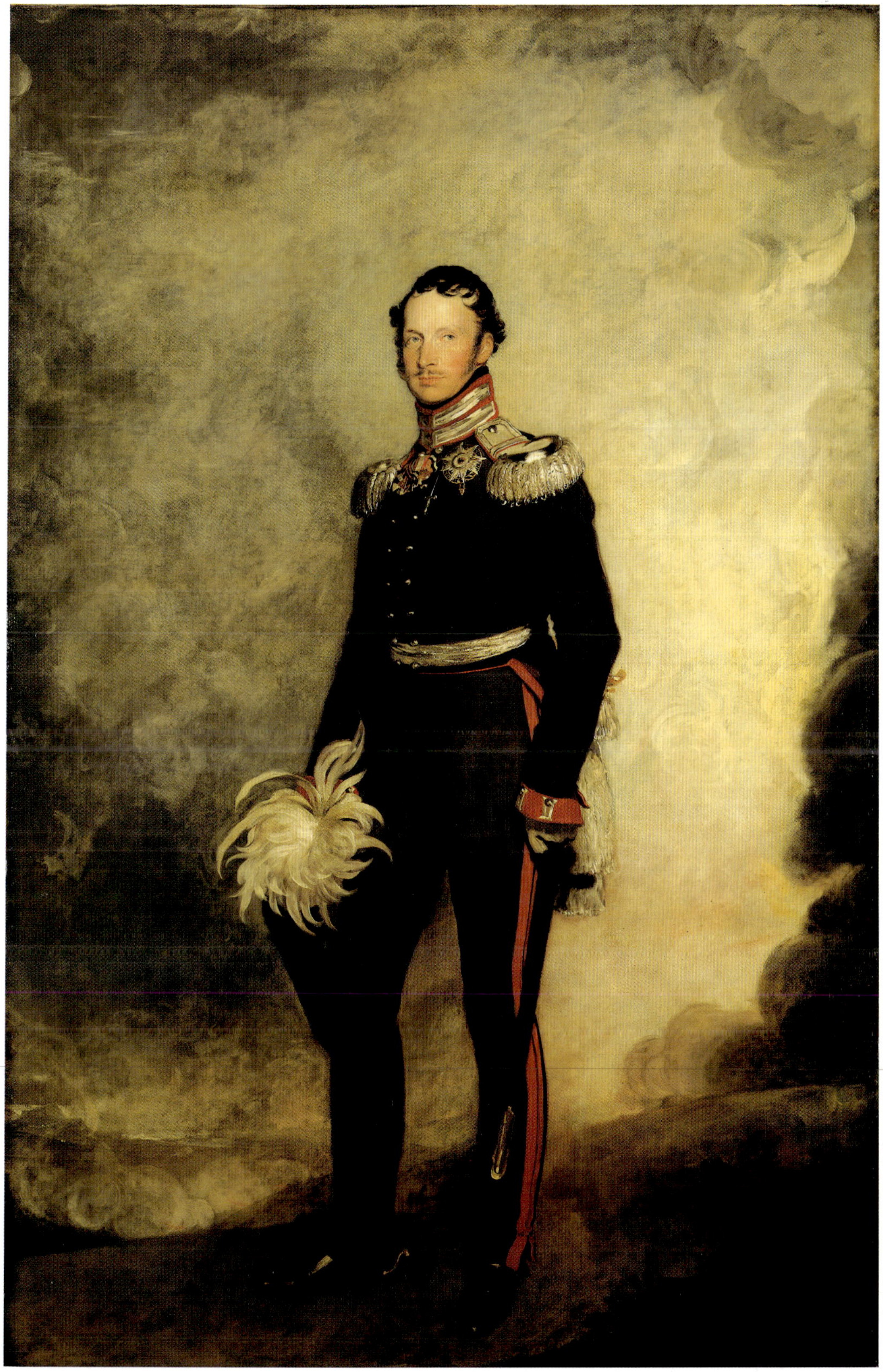

38 **Joannes, Count Capo D'Istria** (1776-1831)
Canvas 51½ x 68¾ in. 1818-19
H.M. the Queen, Waterloo Chamber, Windsor Castle.

This was Lawrence's own favourite amongst the portraits of politicians he painted in Vienna. He wrote to Farington from Vienna in January 1819, 'Count Capo d'Istrias…is the last portrait I have painted here, and fortunately the best'.

Russian Foreign Secretary at the Congress of Vienna, Capo D'Istria became President of the brand new Republic of Greece in 1827. He was assassinated four years later.

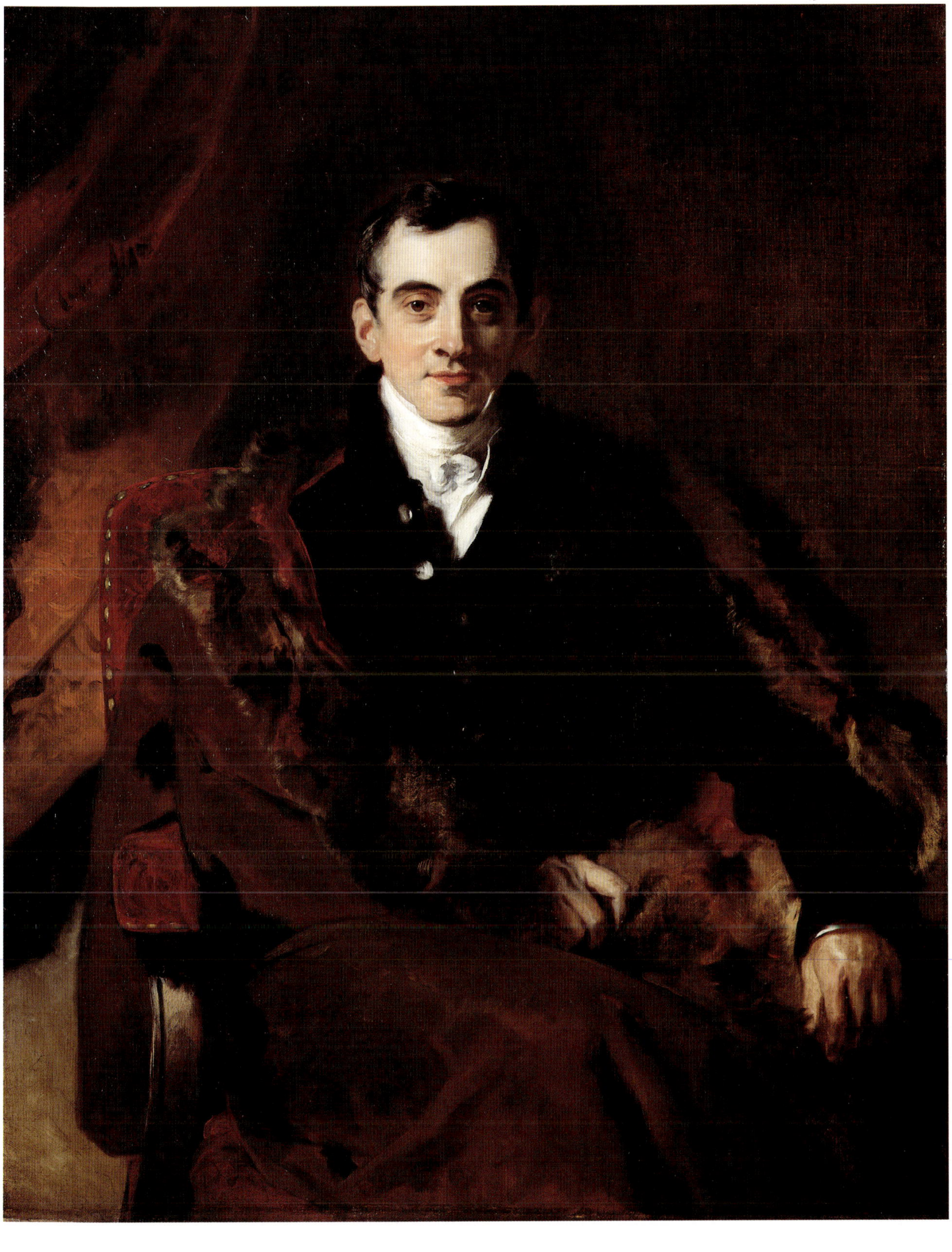

39 **Ercole, Cardinal Consalvi** (1757-1824)
Oil on canvas 105¼ x 68⅗ in. 1819
H.M. the Queen, Waterloo Chamber,
Windsor Castle.

Appointed Cameriere Segreto to Pope Pius VI in 1785 and Secretary of State to Pope Pius VII in 1800, Consalvi became the Pope's closest confidant and advisor. He arranged Lawrence's stay at the Palazzo del Quirinale in 1819. In this portrait, painted in Rome, we can see on the table a bound volume, Consalvi's plan for the reorganisation of administration, law and public finances in the Papal states, published in 1816. In the background St. Peter's is clearly recognisable.

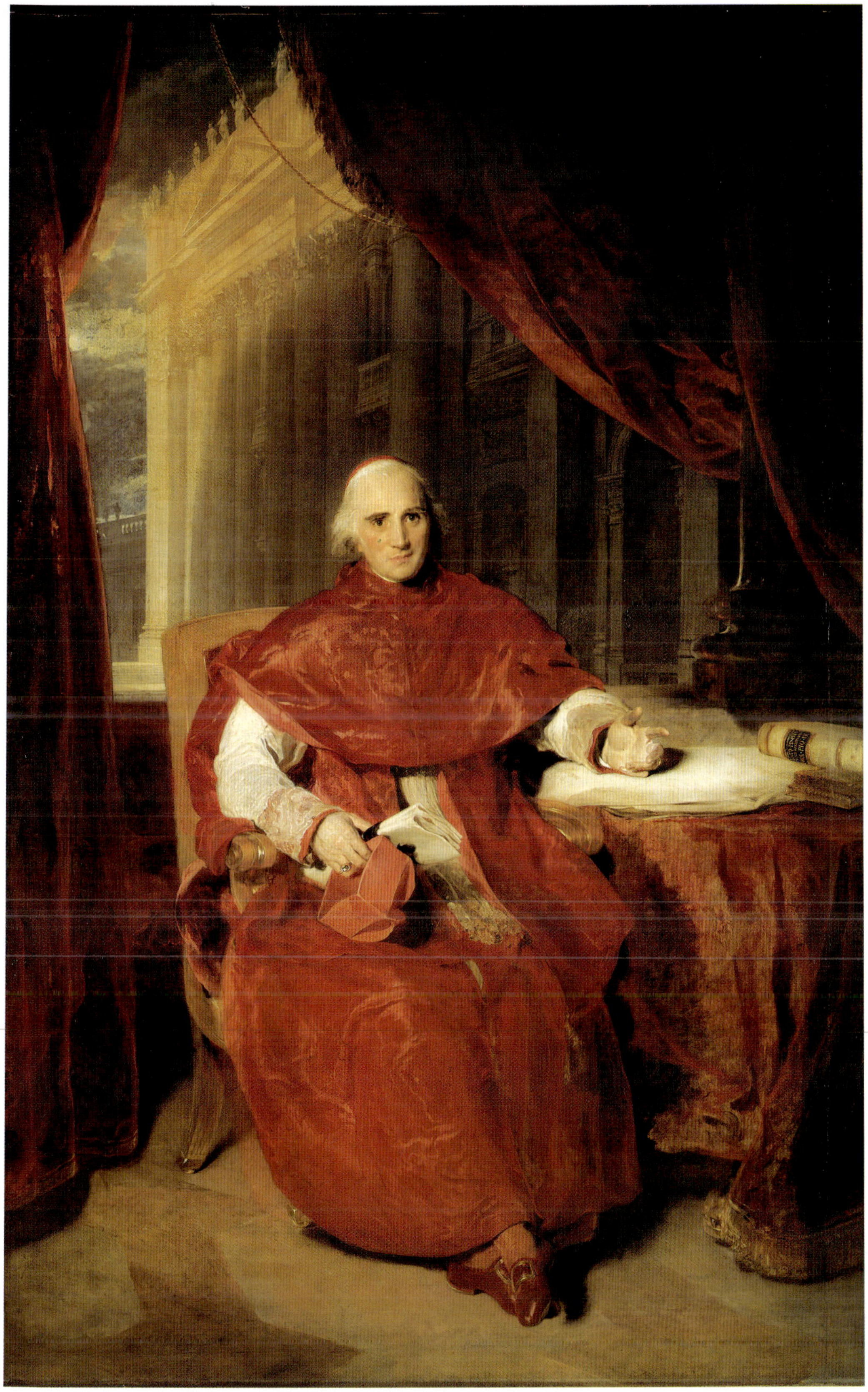

40 **Pope Pius VII** (1742-1823)
Canvas 106 x 70 in. 1819
H.M. the Queen, Waterloo Chamber, Windsor Castle.

Luigi Barnaba Chiaramonti was elected Pope in 1800. He attended Napoleon's Coronation in 1804 but later excommunicated him for annexing the Papal States. Like many of the Papal treasures, including the Apollo Belvedere and the Laocoon shown in the picture, Pius was incarcerated in France and freed by the allied armies in 1814.

The portrait emphasises the Pope's patronage of the arts. In his left hand he holds a document, which may be that by which the sculptor Canova was created Marchese d'Ischia. Over his right shoulder his new sculpture gallery for the Vatican Museum is visible.

In one of his long letters to Farington from Rome, dated 2 July 1819, Lawrence forgets his usual self-effacement, 'If what I have done here in the portrait of the Pope and the Cardinal, be compared only with my own works, I have had complete success; and may truly say so to so near a friend, that as an artist, I have nowhere been more popular than in Rome. I came here too with very moderate expectations; and with many apprehensions, indeed of failure, as to impression on the public mind; and this result is therefore the more pleasing. With the subject of these pictures all here were acquainted; and one of them had been, it was thought, very successfully painted by David and Cammucini, the two first painters of Paris and Rome. The reputation of the former you well know, and the latter is an able artist, and from his character and manners deservedly esteemed. His portrait of the Pope generally pleased: it was exceedingly well drawn, and with a very forcible effect; but he did not encounter the difficulties of his subject. He chose, if I may say so, its too obvious and quiescent character. His view of the face was nearly a profile, with eyes, and head, and frame bending down – an image of respectable decay. I have painted him full in front, with all but the eyes immediately directed to you, with every detail of his countenance, (and it is one of many minute parts, but these animated with benevolence, and a sort of mild energy, that is the real character of his intellect and nature). The securing this, with a good and true tone of colour, has given me undisputed victory'.

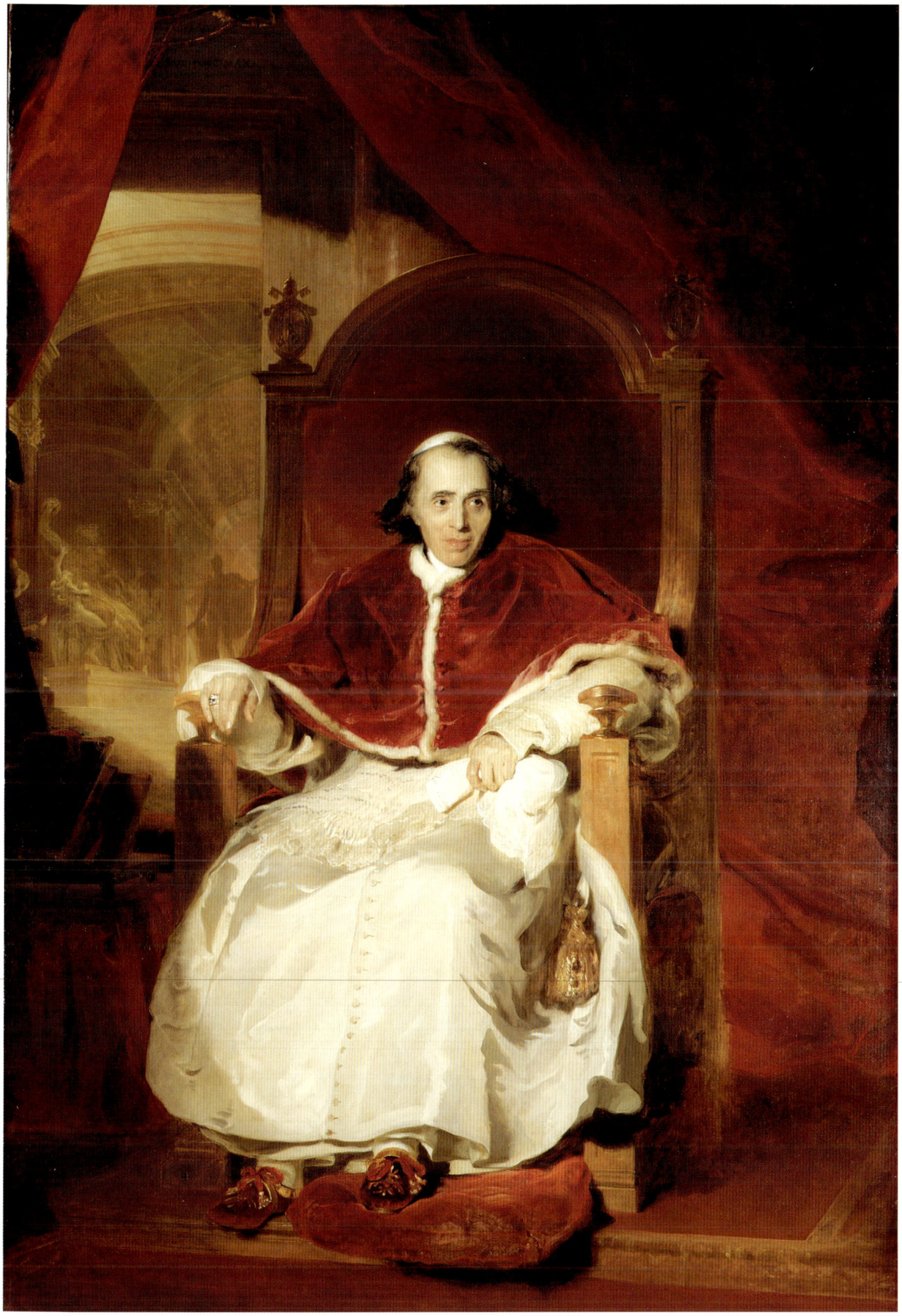

41 **Margaret, Countess of Blessington** (1789-1849)
Canvas 36 x 26¾ in. *c* 1821
The Wallace Collection, London

The Countess of Blessington lived an extraordinary – and scandalous – life. Born Sally Power (christened Margaret) at Knockbrit, County Tipperary, she was married at fifteen to the alcoholic Captain Maurice St. Leger Farmer. It was not long before his abusive behaviour drove her back to her family. She later went to live with the mother and sister of Captain Thomas Jenkins, whose mistress she became. However it was Charles John Gardiner, First Earl of Blessington whom, after her first husband died – accidentally falling from the window at a drunken orgy – she married in 1818.

The couple moved to St. James's Square in London but her reputation preceded her and she was duly snubbed by her female contemporaries. This did not put off the many distinguished male visitors who continued to visit the Blessingtons at their London home, and it was at this time Lady Blessington began her writing career with volumes of essays, novels and a travel book.

In 1823 the couple set out on a tour of Europe and were joined in Paris by Alfred, Count D'Orsay, a previous acquaintance, thought to be the Countess' lover. Travelling to Genoa, they met Lord Byron and it was from this encounter that her famous Conversations with Lord Byron arose. Settling eventually in Italy, the young Count contracted a marriage with the Earl's sixteen-year-old daughter from his first marriage, Lady Harriet Gardiner. It is interesting to note that Blessington insisted, as a clause to the contract, that the marriage not be consummated for four years. Whether due to her own relations with d'Orsay, or to protect the young bride-to-be, or both, it is difficult to say. They moved to Paris in 1828, but in May 1829 the Earl's sudden death left Margaret with severe financial difficulties, as well as heartfelt grief. She returned to London with the d'Orsays. Her association with the Count was, however, the source of even more scandal and was later perceived as having led to the breakdown of the d'Orsays' marriage.

With no choice but to draw on her own talents to make ends meet and, particularly, to fund d'Orsay's supremely extravagant lifestyle, Blessington turned definitively to writing. This did not prevent her from entertaining and her drawing room was the centre of London literary life. Her friends included Byron, Dickens, Thackeray and Disraeli. Despite her circle being exclusively male, she was a strong supporter of younger female writers.

In 1849, with the wolves finally at the door, Blessington and d'Orsay fled to Paris. Her home at Gore House, along with its less modest contents, were auctioned off. The couple found an unprepossessing flat but only two days after moving in Lady Blessington was to die of a heart attack. She was buried in a mausoleum in Chambourcy, planned by Count d'Orsay.

A quote from her letters captures the independence of spirit, and indeed the survival instinct, of the young Irish girl who refused to be beaten by hypocritical London society: 'I am now an old woman, and I have never for a moment repent the the independent line of conduct I have adopted.'

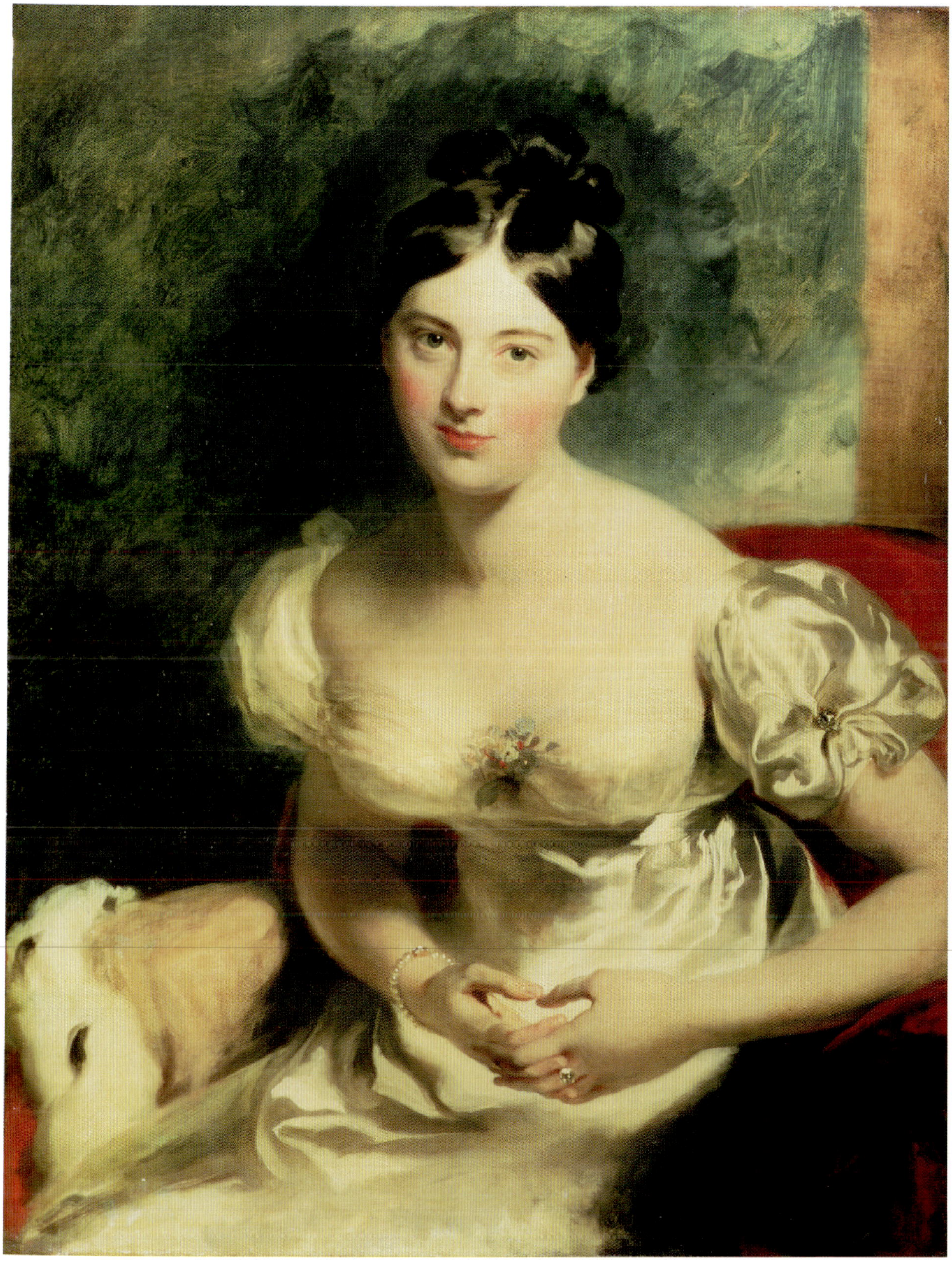

42 **The Honorable George James Welbore Agar-Ellis, MP, FRS, FSA, later 1st Baron Dover** (1797-1833)
Canvas 36 x 29 in. 1823-4
Yale Centre for British Art, New Haven, Connecticut

Only son of the 2nd Viscount Clifden, Agar-Ellis was an influential figure in the art world, and was amongst those who persuaded the government to purchase for the nation in 1824 John Julius Angerstein's collection of Old Master paintings, concerned as he was for the paintings' welfare, which formed the core of the new National Gallery, of which he became trustee in 1827. He was created Baron Dover in 1831 and published in 1832 *The Life of Frederick the Second, King of Prussia* and an edition of Horace Walpole's letters in 1833. In this compelling portrait Lawrence has painted the sitter as both thoughtful and charismatic. The wonderful loose painting of the jacket is strikingly contemporary. Agar-Ellis clearly had great respect for Lawrence and was a pall-bearer at the painter's funeral.

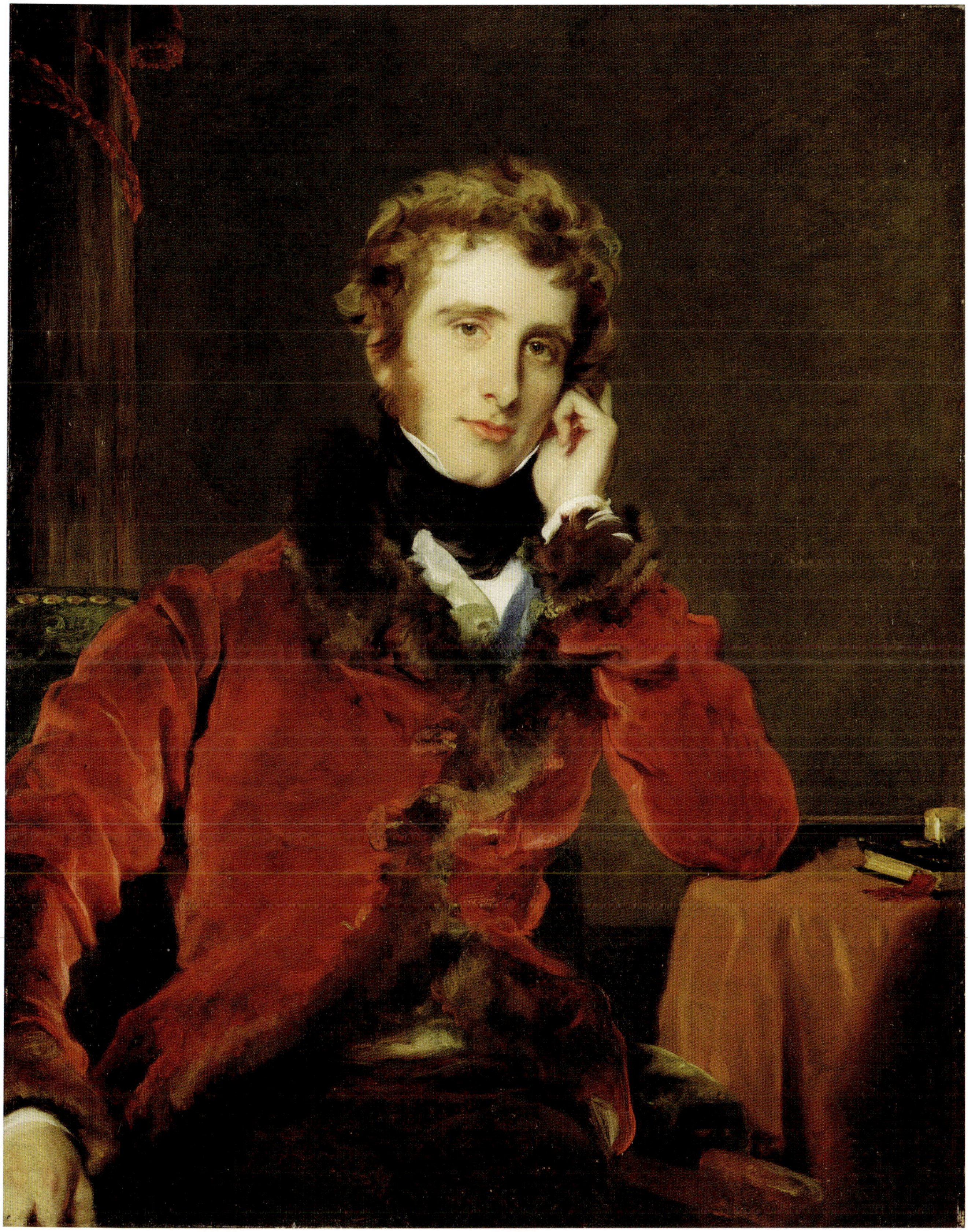

43 **The Calmady Children**
(Emily Calmady, 1818-1906, and Laura Anne Calmady, 1820-94)
Canvasin. $30\frac{7}{8}$ x $30\frac{1}{8}$ in. 1823-4 RA 1824 (99)
The Metropolitan Museum of Art, New York

The daughters of Charles Biggs Calmady of Langdon Hall, Devonshire. Neither married in their lifetimes. Lawrence made a reduction from his usual fee for the children's mother, who had been encouraged by the engraver F.C. Lewis to have them sit for Lawrence. He has unusually initialled the work. According to Sir Michael Levey, the composition may have been inspired by Italian sixteenth and seventeenth century paintings of the Christ Child with St. John the Baptist 'and the ultimate inspiration probably lies in Raphael's *Madonna della Sedia*'. The result can look cloying and sentimental to contemporary eyes. It was however clearly popular at the time; when in 1825 Lawrence took the work to France colour prints were made from it, copies of which were to be found in numerous provincial households.

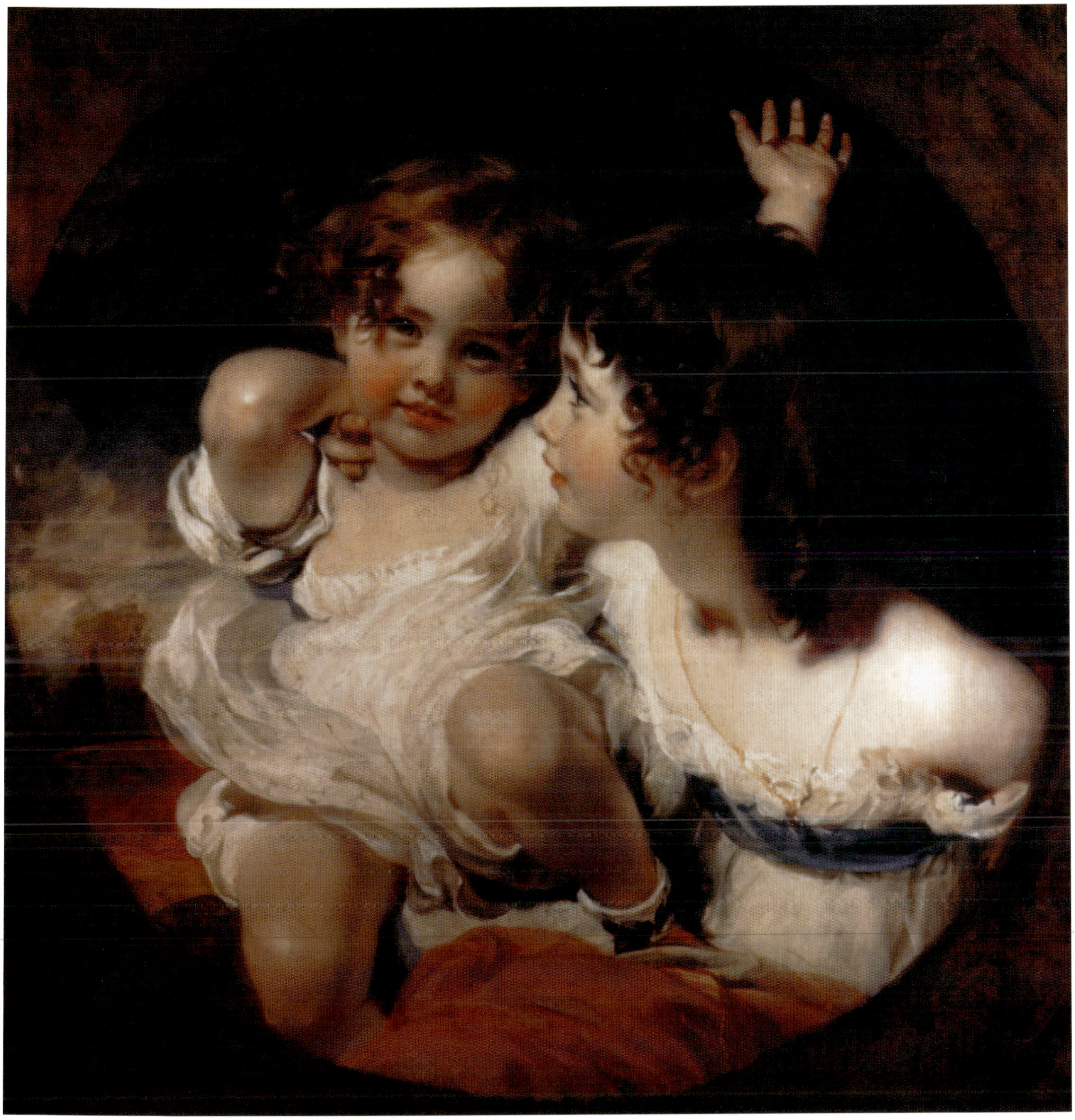

44 **Henry Brougham, 1st Baron Brougham and Vaux** (1778-1868) Canvas 45 x 33½ in. 1825
National Portrait Gallery, London.

Brougham's 'gaunt ungainly figure and ungraceful habit of action' are not particularly obvious in Lawrence's striking yet subdued portrait of him. The straightforward and uncompromising gaze typifies one of the most accomplished speakers of the early nineteenth century.

Brougham was born in Edinburgh, helping to found the *Edinburgh Review* in 1802 and practising as an advocate before moving south to London where he was called to the bar in 1808 and entered Parliament in 1810. He acquired a considerable reputation as a defence counsel, often arguing notorious cases such as that of Queen Caroline at her trial in 1820. A moderate Whig, Brougham instituted many legal and social reforms. He was particularly concerned with education and in 1825, the year in which this portrait seems to have been painted, he was elected Lord Rector of Glasgow University and published a pamphlet entitled 'Observations on the Education of the People'. He was made Lord Chancellor and elevated to the peerage in 1830. As Lord Chancellor he drove about in a specially designed carriage, the first brougham, and his annual residence in Cannes prompted its development from a fishing village into the Brighton of the Côte d'Azur.

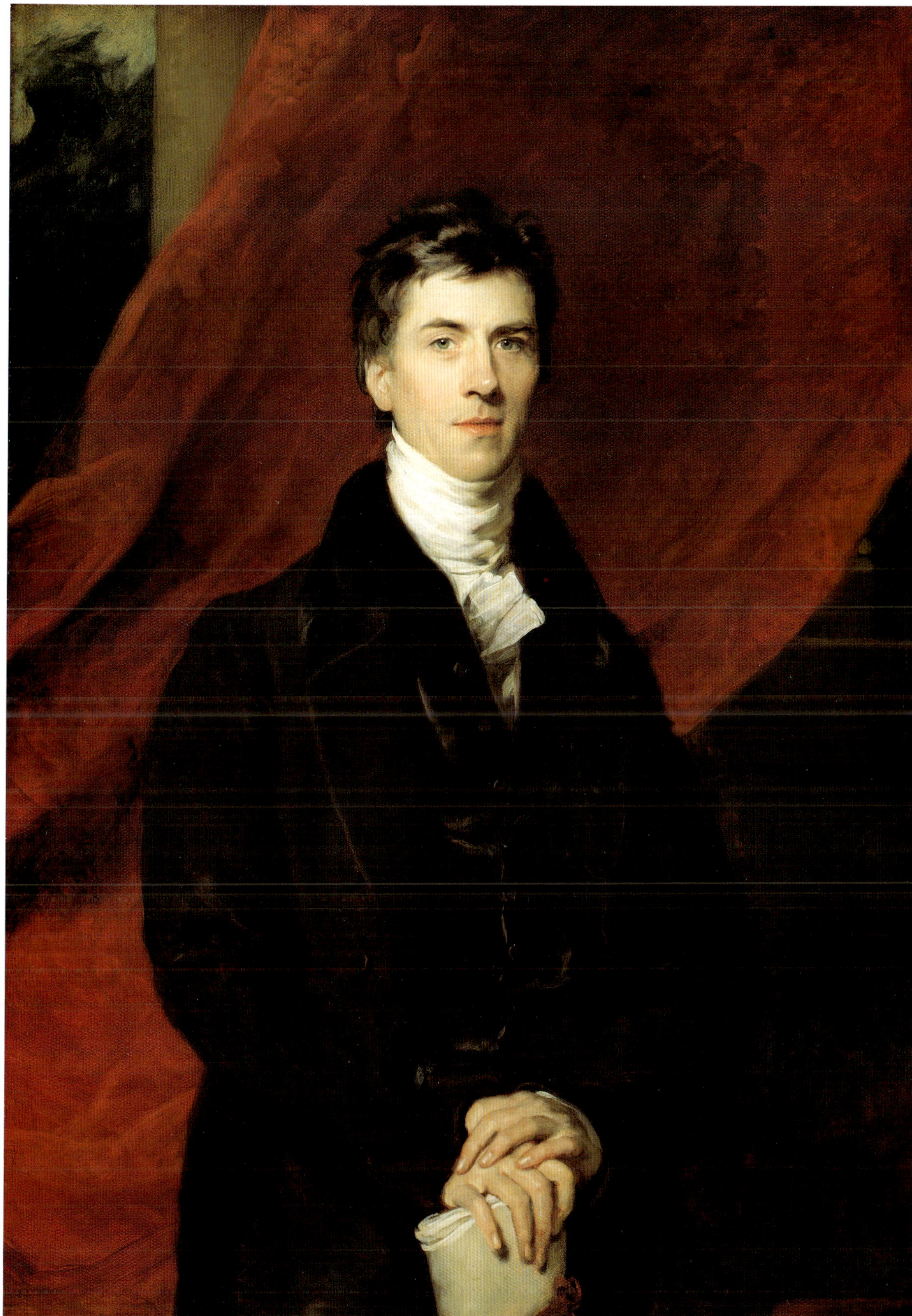

45 **Henry Fuseli, RA** (1741-1825)
Canvas 56 x 43 in. 1825
Musée Bonnat, Bayonne

Fuseli was the son of a portrait painter, Johann Caspar Füssli. Originally trained as a priest, Reynolds encouraged his artistic talent and he became an accomplished painter and draughtsman, as well as a writer on art. Swiss-born, he worked mainly in England where he was an outstanding member of the Romantic Movement. His erotic masterpiece *The Nightmare* sealed his reputation when shown at the Royal Academy in 1782. He was Professor of Painting there from 1799-1805 and again in 1810 and Keeper in 1804-25. He is chiefly known for his work illustrating Shakespeare and Milton, and his paintings, which explored horror and fantasy, were much admired by Blake. The Surrealists would later look to his work as an influence.

Fuseli sat for Lawrence in 1825 and the work was unfinished at the time of Lawrence's death. The painting was subsequently completed by John Jackson.

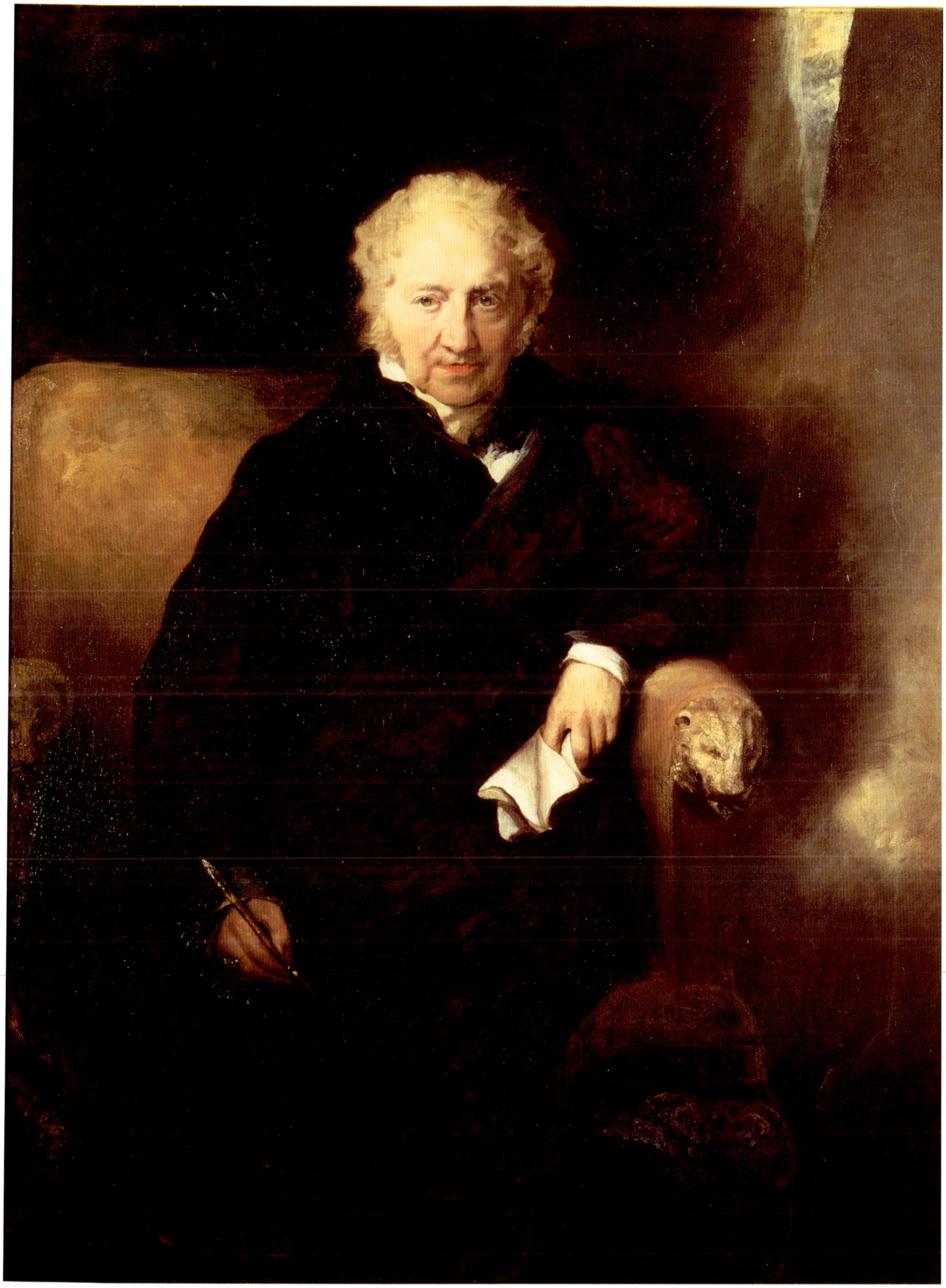

46 **Charles William Lambton (Master Lambton)**
(1818-31)
Canvas 54 x 44 in. RA 1825 (288)
Coll: Lord Lambton.

Master Lambton was originally dressed in yellow. He is seated, not in an enormous armchair but in a rocky bower. He muses by moonlight. This beautiful picture has always been widely admired. B.W. Proctor wrote to Lawrence whilst the picture was in progress.

' What a beautiful boy that is of Lambton's. Pray do not forget or neglect your yesterday's intention of lifting him above the level of a portrait. I really think that you need fear nothing old or new which can be placed beside it. It will put a feather (as the saying is) into your cap, which is so full of feathers already'.

Charles William Lambton, who died when he was thirteen, was the eldest son of John George Lambton, created Earl of Durham in 1833 and Governor-General of Canada in 1838, and his second wife, Lady Louisa Elizabeth Grey, second daughter of the 2nd Earl Grey.

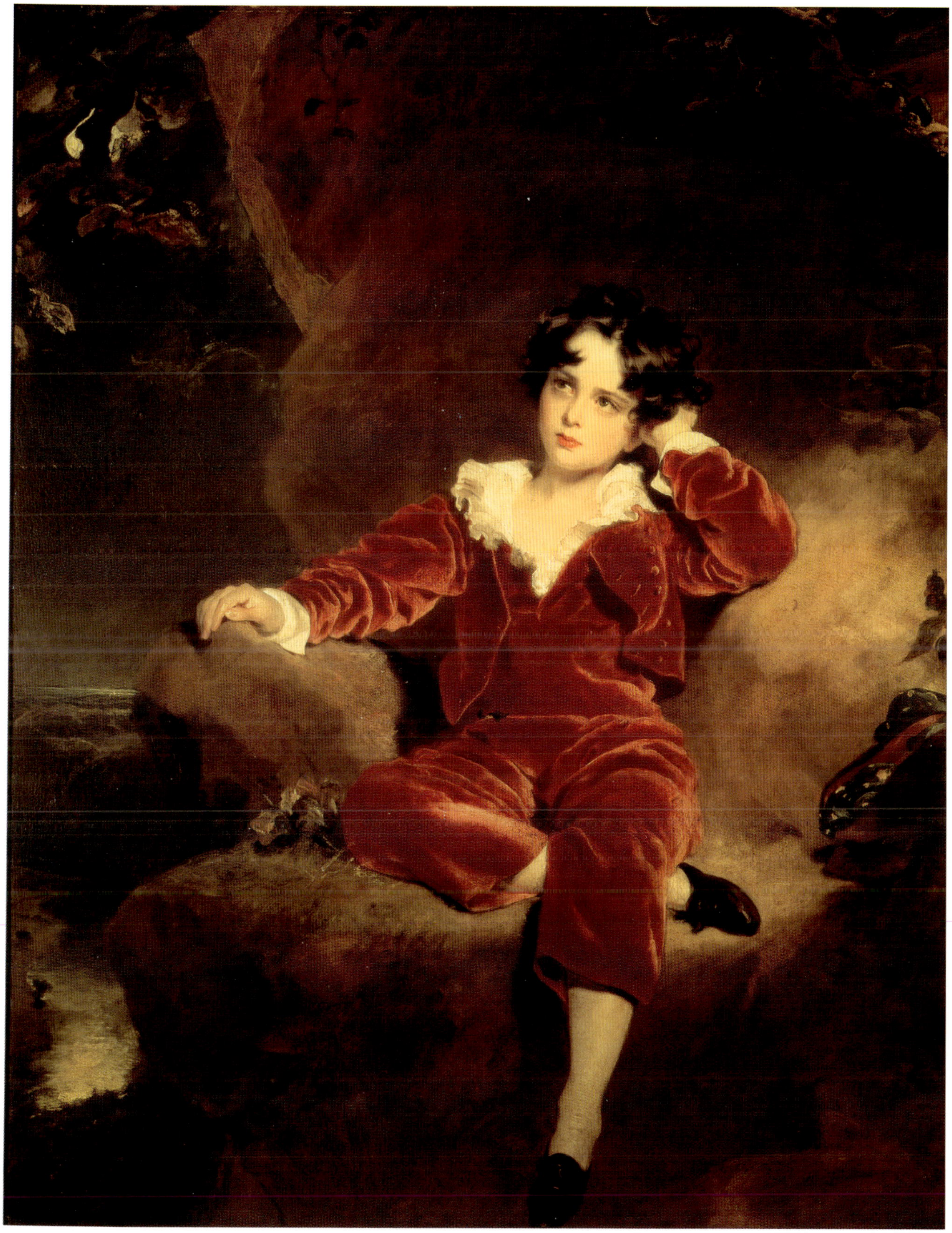

47 **Louisa Georgina Augusta Anne Murray**
(1822-1891)
Canvas 53½ x 42½ in. RA 1826 (396)
Iveagh Bequest, Kenwood House, London.

Miss Murray was the daughter of General Sir George Murray and Lady Louisa Erskine who omitted to get married until 1826 – the year in which the portrait was exhibited – after the death of her first husband, Sir James Erskine, the year before. The young Louisa would marry Henry Boyce in 1843.

There are several repetitions and a number of engravings of what was evidently a popular picture.

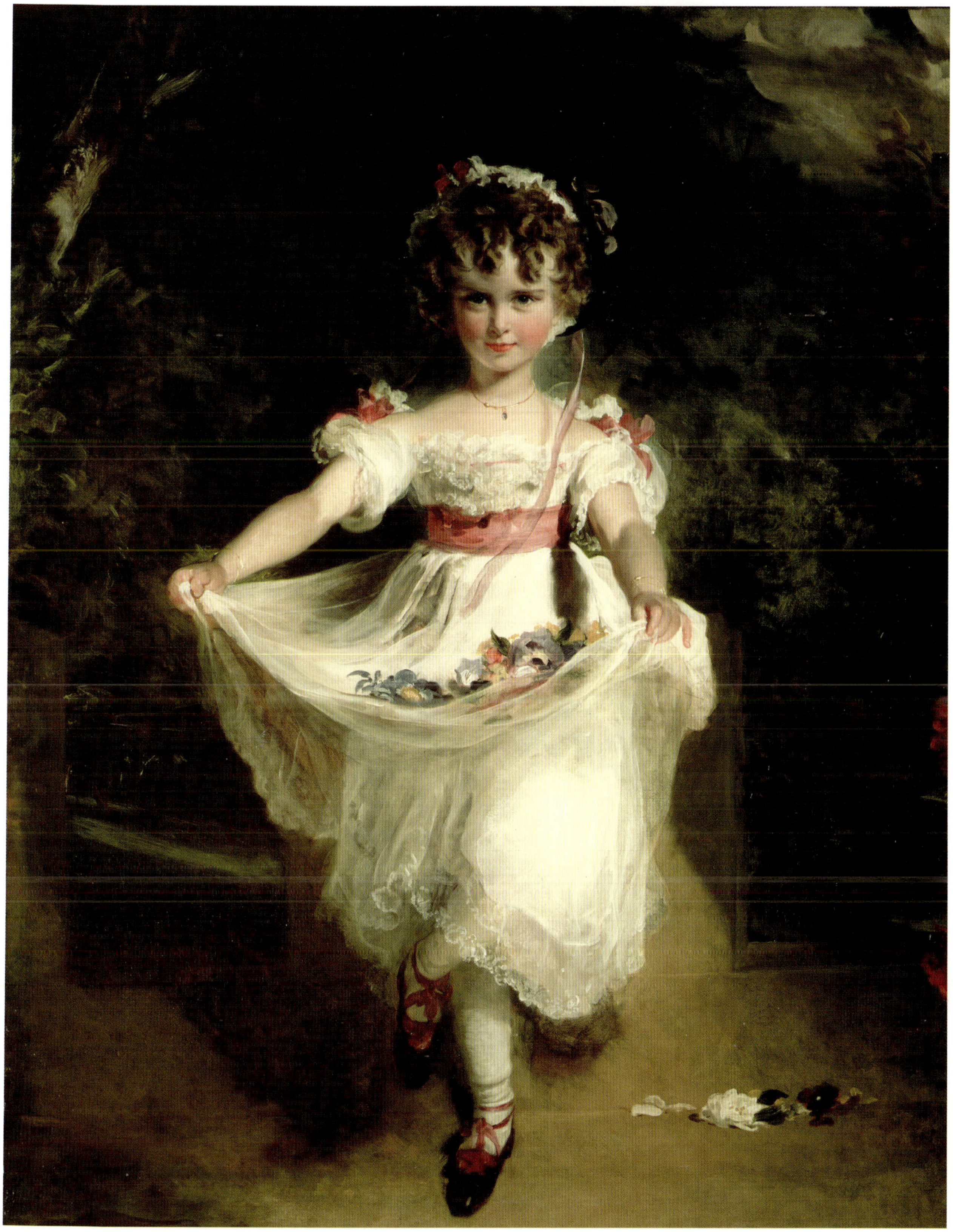

48 **George Canning, MP** (1770-1827)
Canvas 94 x 58 in. RA 1826 (109)
National Portrait Gallery, London.

The last of Lawrence's four portrait types of Canning. The first was painted in 1809 and the second, known in several versions, was shown at the 1810 RA (67). The third type, a full length showing him standing with his arms folded in the House of Commons, was probably painted for Canning himself and was shown at the 1825 RA (83). A three-quarter length version is in the Waterloo Chamber. This portrait precedes and the illustrated portrait follows Lawrence's final trip abroad, in 1825, which Canning helped to organise. He wrote to Lawrence on 29 May 1825.

'I have received this Morning a Letter from the Prince Polignac, announcing the compliance of the King of France and the Dauphin with His Majesty's desire; promising to sit for their Portraits to you, so soon the Fetes etc., shall be over. I have sent this Letter to His Majesty and give you notice of it, that you may be prepared to set out for Paris, when you shall receive His Majesty's commands to that effect'.

Canning entered the House of Commons in 1794 and served under Pitt. He was Foreign Minister in the Portland Tory ministry of 1807 and was instrumental in reopening the Peninsula War. His quarrel with Castlereagh over the latter's conduct of the war on several fronts led to their famous duel on Putney Heath, 21 September 1809. Kept out of office until Castlereagh's death, Canning returned to the Foreign Office in 1822 where he established the foundations of British foreign policy for the whole of the nineteenth century. He was appointed Prime Minister and Chancellor of the Exchequer just before his death in 1827.

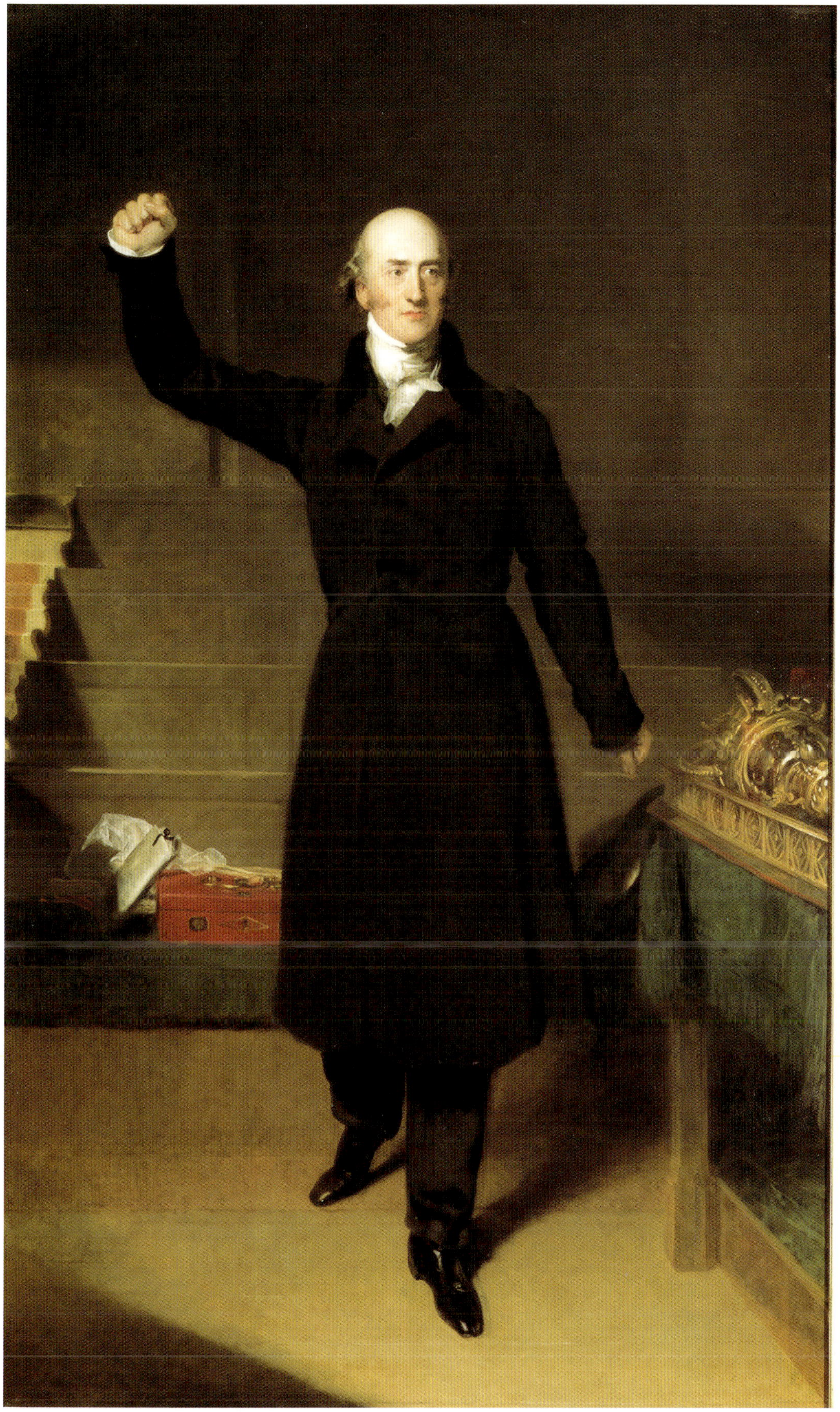

49 **Lady Caroline Lamb** (1785-1828)
Canvas 21 x 18½ in. *c.* 1827
Bristol City Museum and Art Gallery, UK

Caroline was the only daughter of Lord Duncannon and his wife Lady Henriette. Caroline lived her early years at Devonshire House, the home of Georgiana, Duchess of Devonshire. The house was the centre of Whig politics and here Caroline met Charles Fox and William Melborne amongst many others. William was attracted to Caroline and they married when she was seventeen.

The marriage started well – indeed Caroline is said to have been besotted – but William's parliamentary ambitions meant that they spent less time together which, given Caroline's nature, seemingly both insecure and volatile, inevitably harmed their relationship.

In 1812 Lady Lamb met Byron when he was at the beginning of his fame and, as noted earlier, began a wild and highly visible affair. She is well remembered for remarking that Byron was 'mad, bad and dangerous to know'. The affair lasted four months, after which it was ended by Byron. After their final split she began writing the novel *Glenarvon*, supposedly an apology to him. It was not accepted as such, painting him as it did in such a dark light, and her marriage was left in ruins.

In this portrait Caroline looks much younger than she was at the time of its painting, although she was always said to have had a childlike air. She died before the portrait was completed and the clouds surrounding her head, probably a reference to her death, also seem to reinforce her ethereal, Romantic and tragic nature.

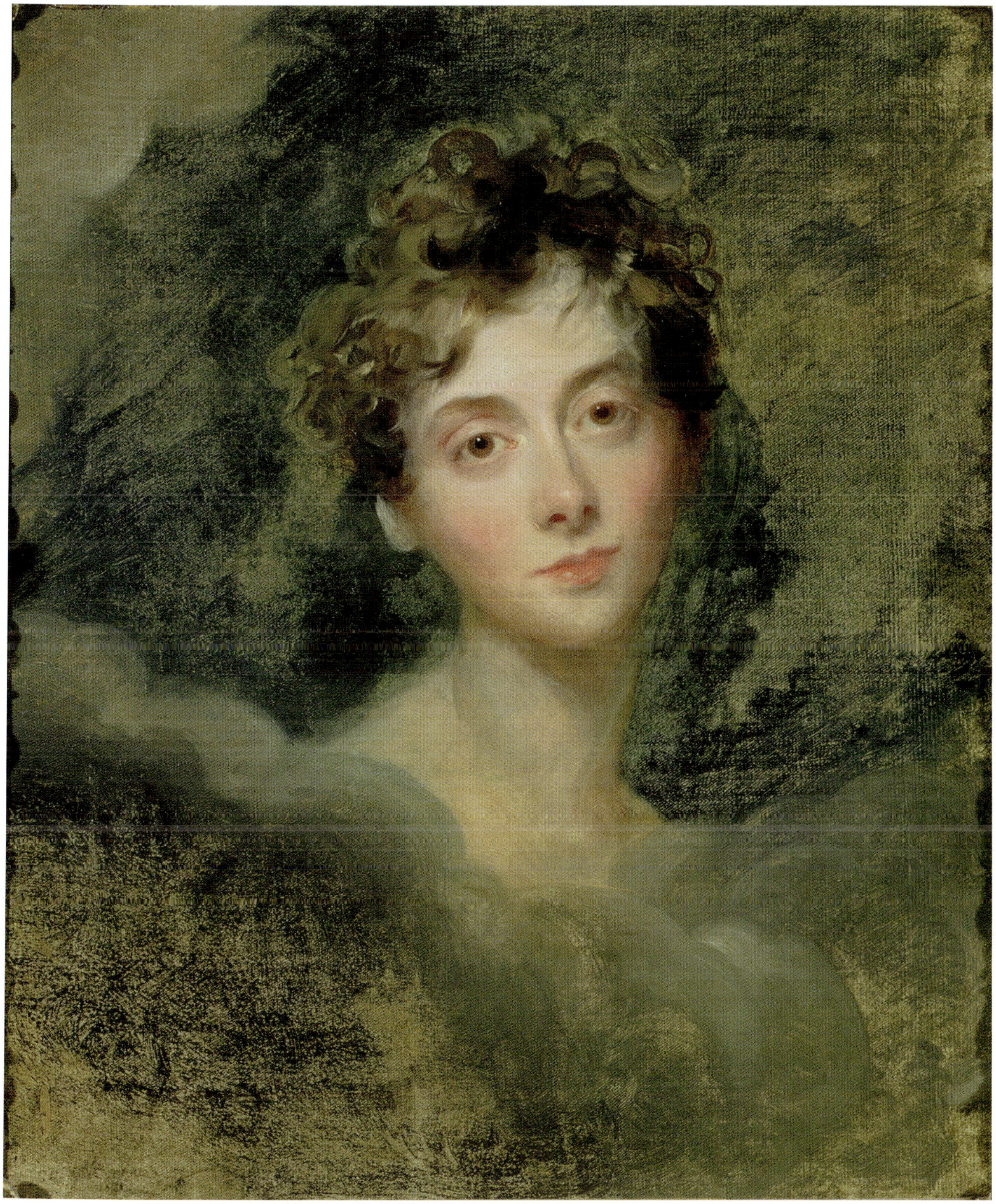

50 **Rosamund Hester Elizabeth Croker** (1810-1906)

Canvas 29½ x 26 in. RA 1827 (26).

Albright-Knox Art Gallery, Buffalo, New York

The twenty-first child of William Pennell, British Consul-General in Brazil, Rosamund Croker was adopted by John Wilson Croker, the politician, her brother-in-law, who was also painted by Lawrence. she married George Barrow, Chief Clerk at the colonial office in 1832. He succeeded his father as 2nd Baronet in 1848.

The portrait was first shown, to much acclaim, at the Royal Academy exhibition of 1827, with one critic remarking, 'men stand before it in a half-circle, admiring its loveliness'. It was one of Lawrence's most popular female portraits as well as one of his most accomplished.

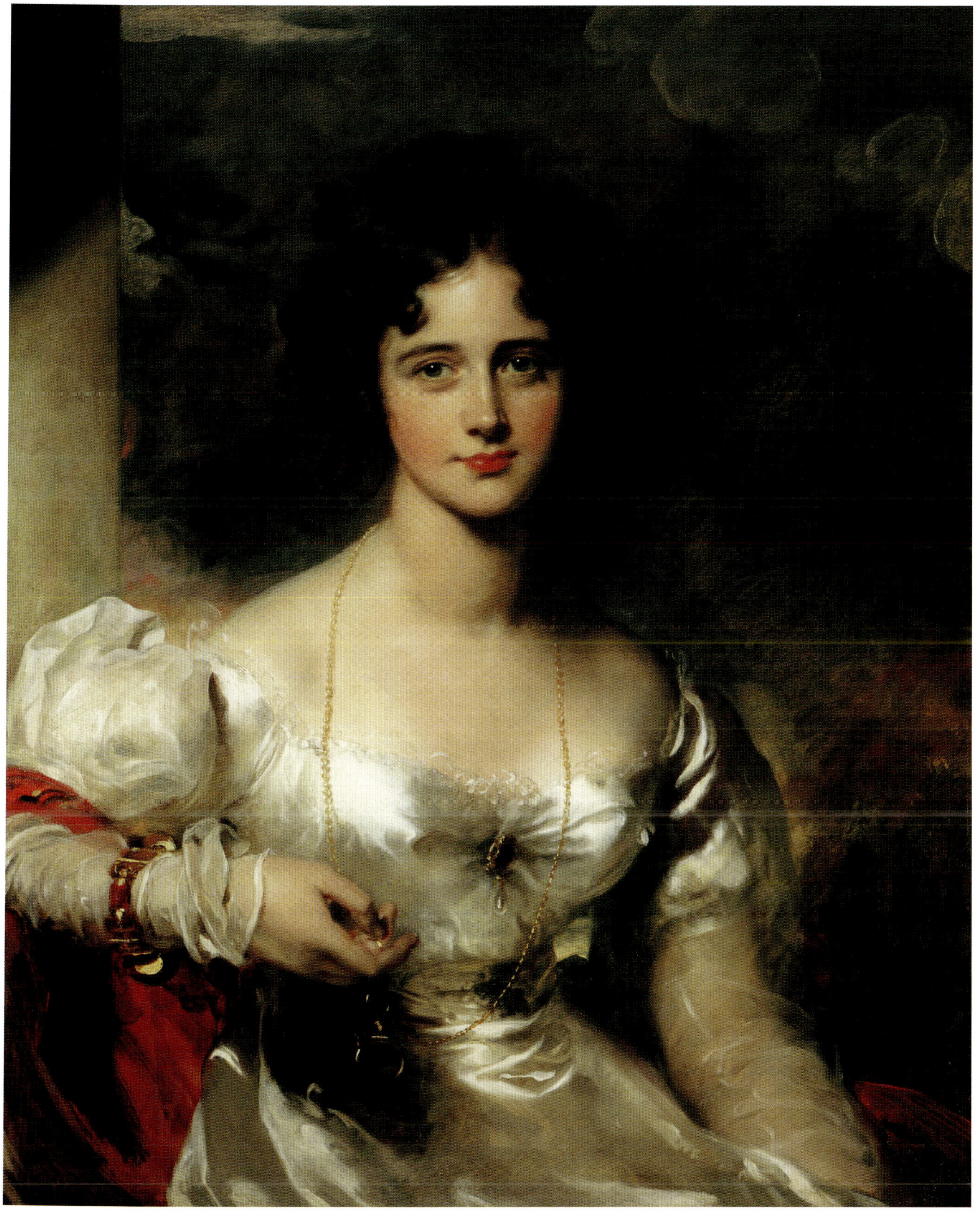

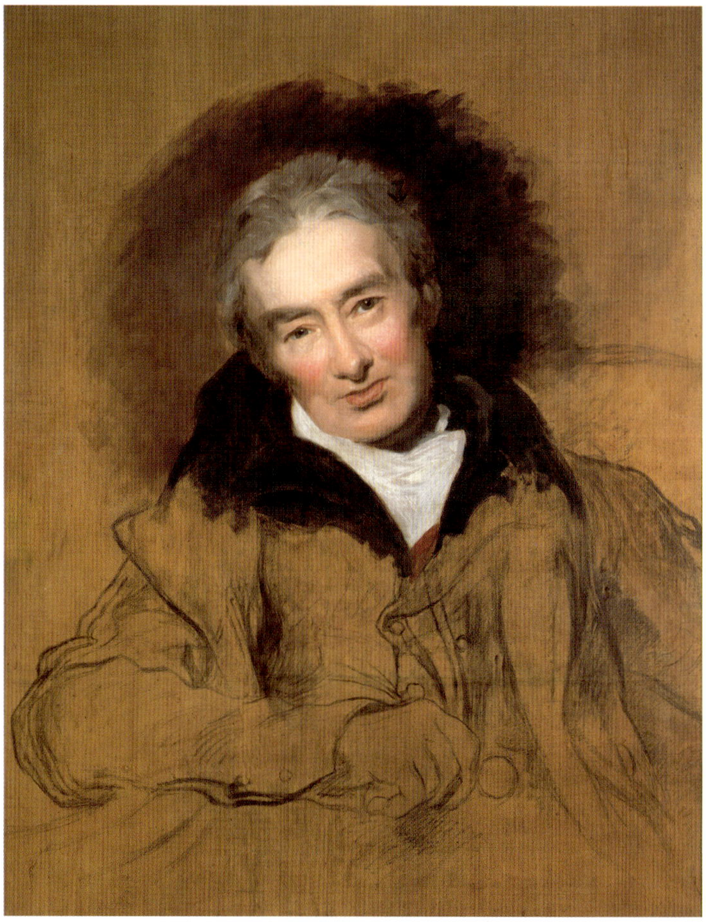

51 **William Wilberforce, MP** (1759-1833)
Canvas. 38½ x 43¾ in. 1828.
National Portrait Gallery, London

This unfinished portrait of the great British social reformer was commissioned by Sir Robert Inglis, and bequeathed to the nation in 1855. Wilberforce campaigned for the abolition of slavery and, in 1807, the Abolition Bill finally passed through the House of Commons. This work was one of over one hundred and fifty portraits left unfinished at the time of Lawrence's death in 1830.

52 **Prince George of Cumberland** (1819-78)
Canvas 99½ x 54½ in. 1828
H.M. the Queen, Buckingham Palace, London

The only child of Ernest Augustus, Duke of Cumberland, later King of Hanover, Prince George was the grandson of George III. He succeeded his father as King George V of Hanover in 1851 but was deposed in 1866. Wearing the star of the Golden Lion of Hesse-Kassel, he stands, with a somewhat precocious air, with Windsor Castle in the back-ground.

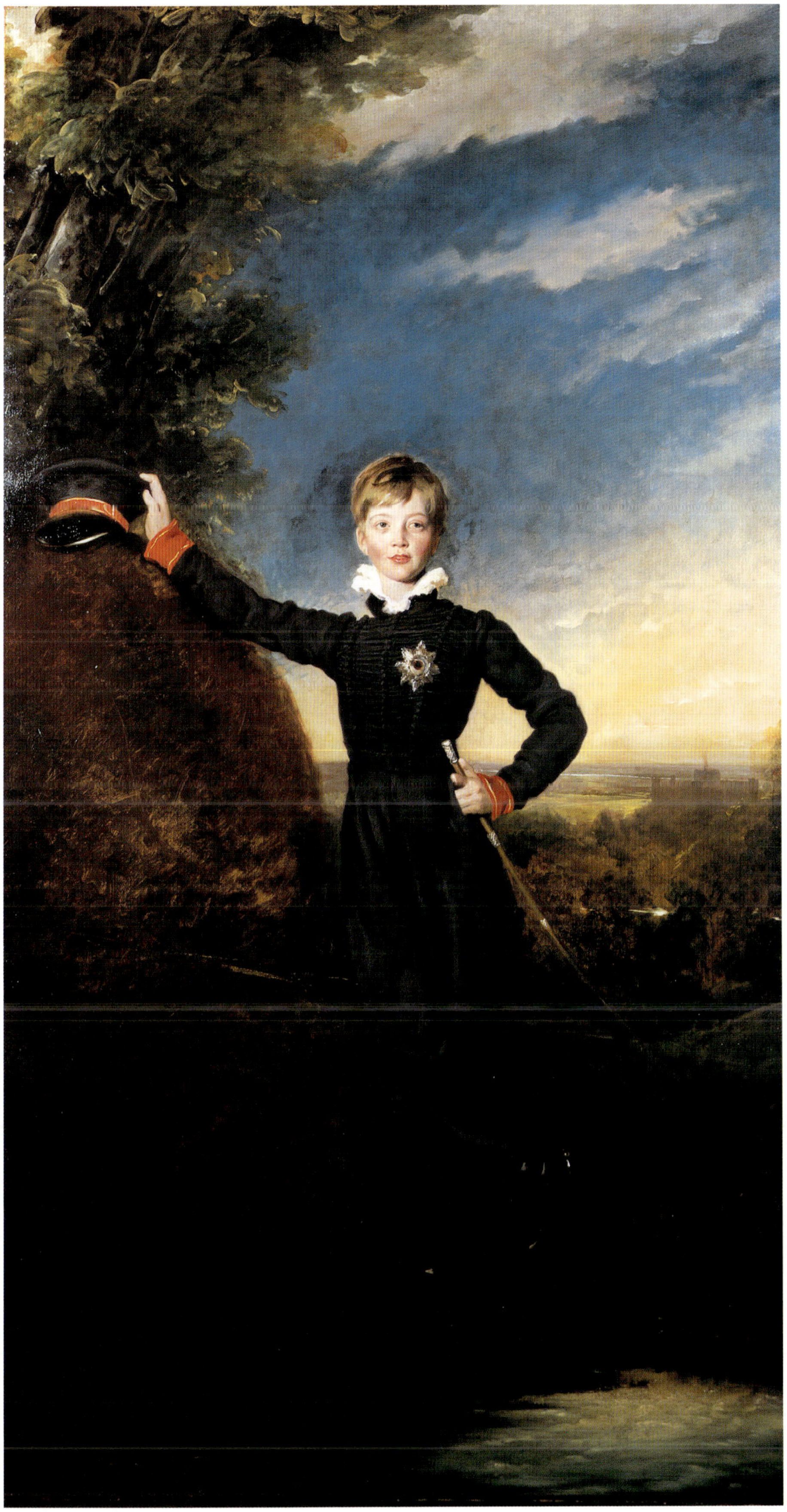

53 **Sir John Soane RA** (1753-1837)
Canvas 56 x 44 in. 1828
Sir John Soane's Museum, London

Sir John Soane was born at Goring-on-Thames near Reading. He was the son of a bricklayer and trained as an architect initially under George Dance the Younger and then Henry Holland.

Soane was awarded a travelling scholarship by the Royal Academy in 1777, spending it in Italy, where he developed a neo-classical style. His work on the exterior of the Bank of England gained him many new commissions including the dining rooms of 10 and 11 Downing Street, the Dulwich Picture Gallery and Pitshanger Manor, Ealing. He was knighted in 1831 and in 1833 by Act of Parliament his own house was made into a National Museum of Architecture.

His house in Lincoln's Inn Fields was also the setting for his antiquities and his works of art. By leaving his house to the nation, he was determined to establish the house as a museum to which both 'amateurs and students' should have access.

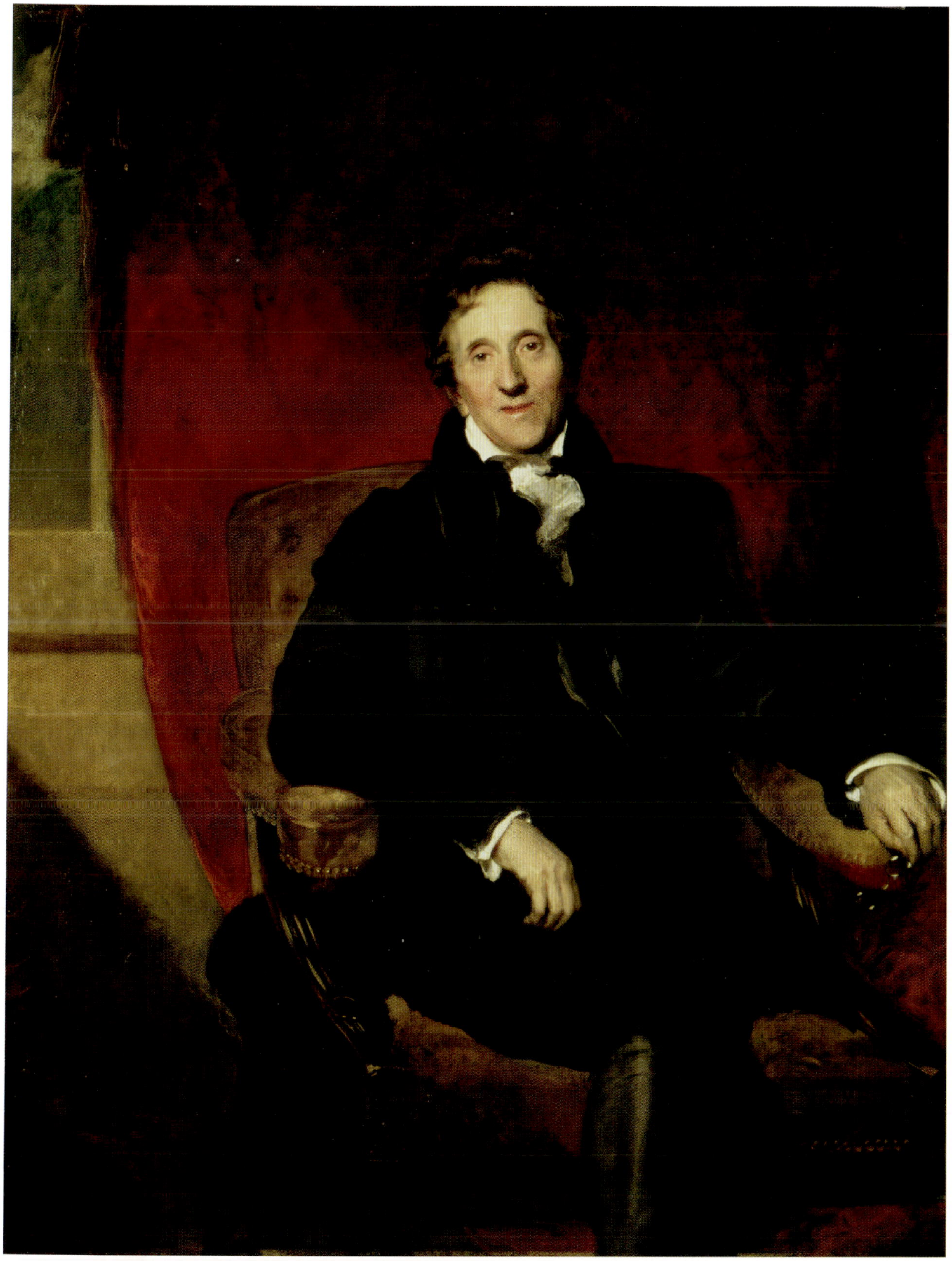

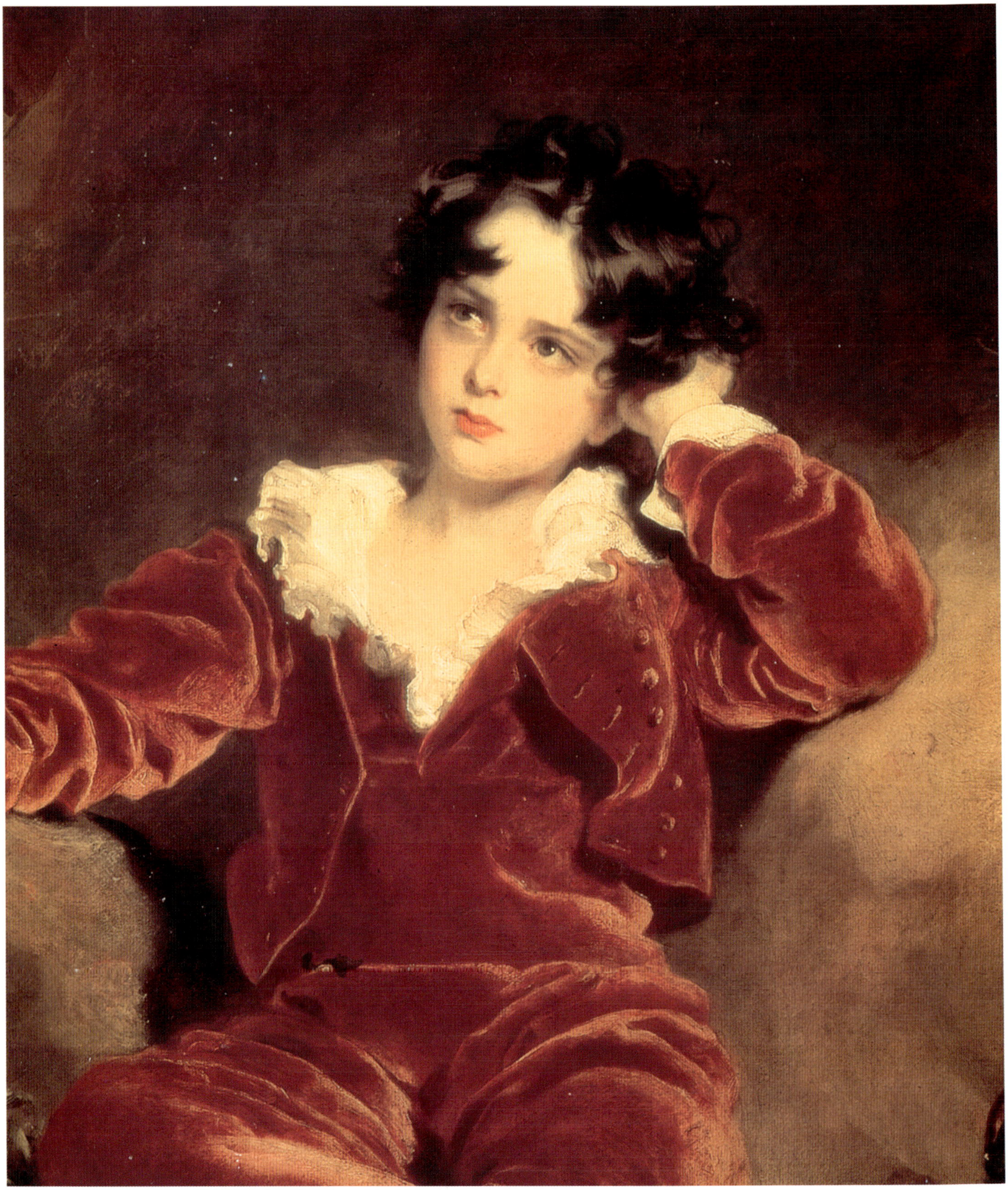

CHRONOLOGY OF THE LIFE AND WORKS OF SIR THOMAS LAWRENCE

(Includes key events in Lawrence's life and lists those of his Royal Academy exhibits which are illustrated in this book.)

1769 13 April.
Thomas Lawrence born in Bristol, fourteenth child of Thomas Lawrence and Lucy Read. Thomas was the youngest of the five children – out of sixteen – who survived.

Thomas Lawrence Snr. resigned his position as Supervisor of Excise to become landlord of 'The White Lion', Bristol.

1773
Family moved to 'The Black Bear', Devizes, on the London to Bath road. Thomas drew portrait sketches of his father's customers.

1779
Family moved to Oxford. Lawrence drew portraits, was commissioned to copy Reynolds' New College Window and had his portrait engraved.

1780
Weymouth and Bath. Lawrence built up a practise in pastel and pencil portraits.

1785
Won a silver gilt palette from the Society of Arts for a copy in crayons after Raphael's *Transfiguration*.

1787
Moved permanently to London.
Address: 4, Leicester Square.
Parents moved to London.
September. Student of oil painting at the Royal Academy for three months.

Exhibited seven works at the Royal Academy, his first. He exhibited at every Royal Academy from 1787 to 1830 excluding 1809, when he had a difference of opinion with the hanging committee, and 1819, when he was in Italy. He always exhibited from five to nine works although he showed only two in 1807.

1788
Address: 41, Jermyn Street.

1790

R.A. 100	Queen Charlotte (Plate 4).
R.A. 171	Elizabeth Farren (Plate 5).

1791
Elected Associate of the Royal Academy.
Address: 24, Old Bond Street.

R.A. 180	Homer Reciting his Poems (Plate 1).

1792
Appointed Painter in Ordinary to the King on the death of Reynolds, and succeeded him as painter to the Dilettanti Society.

R.A. 209	Arthur Atherley (Plate 6).
R.A. 65	George III (Plate 7).

1793
Prices:
Head and shoulders 40 gns;
Half length 80 gns;
Whole length 160 gns.

1794
Elected full Royal Academician.

1795
Address: Piccadilly.

R.A. 131	Charles,1st Earl Grey (Plate 8).
R.A. 75	Sarah Goodwin Moulton, ('Pinkie') (Plate 9).

1796

R.A. 164	Joseph Farington (Plate 10).

1797

May: Death of mother. October: Death of father.

R.A. 74	Henry Cecil, 10th Earl of Exeter and family (Plate 11)
R.A. 170	Satan Summoning his Legions (Plate 13).

1798

Address: 57, Greek Street.

R.A. 225	John Philip Kemble as Coriolanus (Plate 15).

1799

R.A. 137	Samuel Lysons (Plate 16).

1800

R.A. 28	The Children of Ayscoghe Boucherett (Plate 17).

1801

R.A. 187	John Philip Kemble as Hamlet (Plate 20).

1802

R.A. 72	Caroline Princess of Wales and Princess Charlotte (Plate 21).

1807

Prices:
Head and shoulders 50 gns;
Kitcat 70 gns;
Half length 100 gns;
Bishops' Half Length 120 gns;
Whole length 200 gns.

R.A. 210	Sir Francis Baring, 1st. Bart, John Baring and Charles Wall. (Plate 23).

1810

Prices: on a scale rising to 300 gns. for a Whole length.

R.A. 61	Robert Stewart, Viscount Castlereagh (Plate 24).

1811

R.A. 113	Benjamin West (Plate 25).

1814

Address: 65, Russell Square.
The Waterloo Chamber portraits project initiated.

1815

Short visit to Paris.
Knighted in preparation for his position as artistic ambassador in Vienna etc.

R.A. 28	Mrs. Jens Wolff (Plate 29).
R.A. 76	Clemens Lothar Wenzel, Prince Metternich (Plate 33).
R.A. 109	Arthur Wellesley, Ist Duke of Wellington (Plate 28).
R.A. 155	Field-Marshal Gebhardt von Blücher (Plate 31).
R.A. 163	Ivanovitch, Count Platov (Plate 32).

1818

September. Aix-la-Chapelle to paint the East European Monarchs.
December. Vienna to paint the members of the Congress.
Prices: paid 500 gns. for each whole length and 300 gns. for the smaller pictures.

1819
May. Rome to paint Pope Pius VII and Cardinal Consalvi.

1820
March. Returned to England.
President of the Royal Academy on the death of Benjamin West.

1821

R.A. 99	The Calmady Children (Plate 43).

1825
France to paint Charles X and the Dauphin.

R.A. 288	Charles William Lambton (Master Lambton)(Plate 46).

1826

R.A. 396	Louisa Georgina Augusta Anne Murray (Plate 47).
R.A. 109	George Canning (Plate 48).

1827

R.A. 26	Rosamund Hester Elizabeth Croker (Plate 50).

1830 7 January.
Death.
20 January.
Funeral and burial in St. Paul's Cathedral.

Prices at death:
Head and shoulders 200 gns;
Kitcat 300 gns;
Half length 400 gns;
Bishop's Half length 500 gns;
Whole length 600 gns;
'Extra' whole length 700 gns.

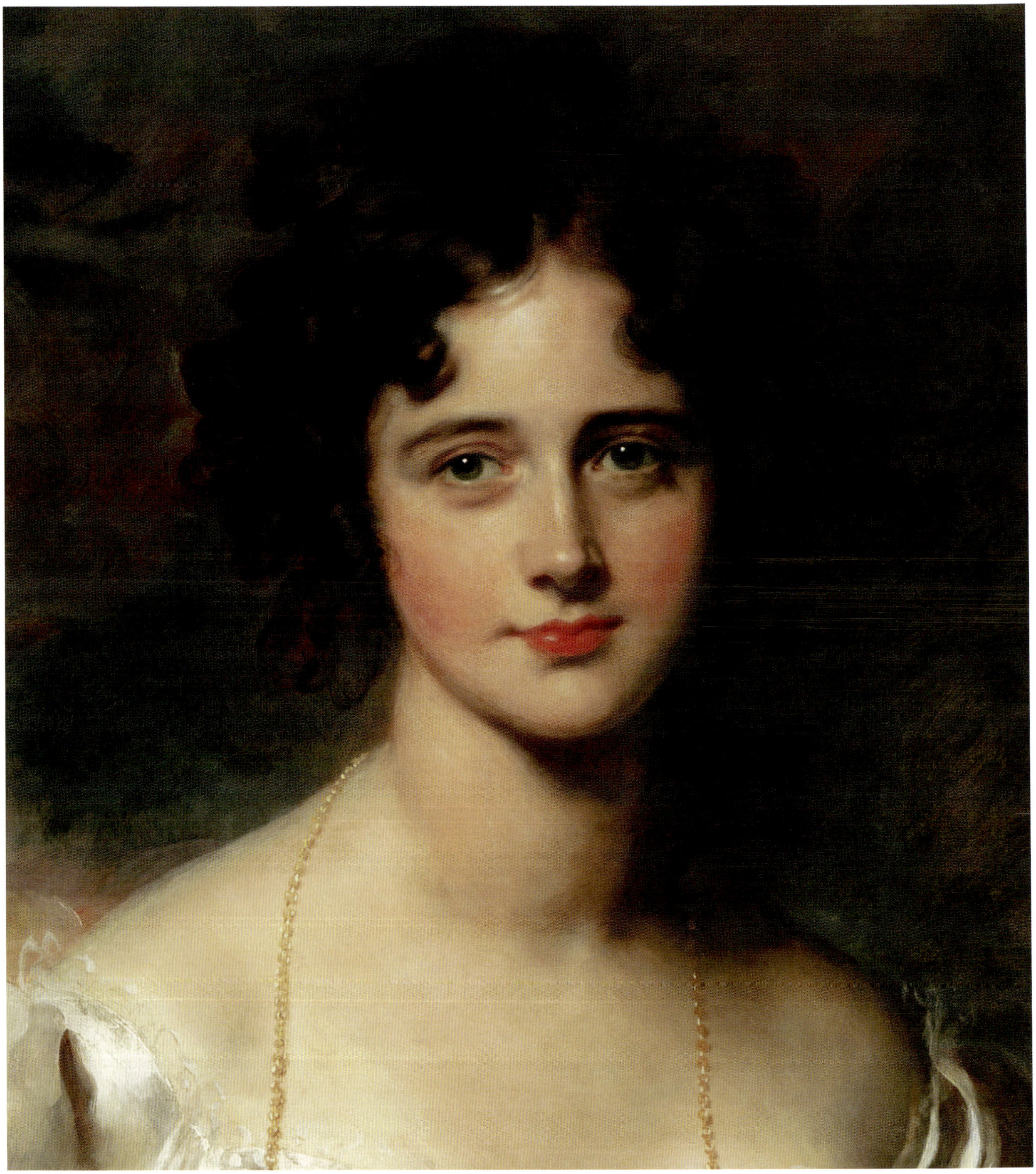

BIBLIOGRAPHY

This bibliography includes only the full-length works on Lawrcncc. Kcnncth Garlick's 1954 biography includes a fuller bibliography and all works on English painting of the late eighteenth and early nineteenth centuries include sections on Lawrence. Oliver Millar's catalogue is included because it contains definitive entries for all the Lawrences in the Royal Collection, including the Waterloo Chamber portraits.

D.E. WILLIAMS — *The Life and Correspondence of Sir Thomas Lawrence Kt.* 2 vols.1831

Lord Ronald SUTHERLAND GOWER — *Sir Thomas Lawrence* 1900
Contains an appendix by Algernon Graves listing all Lawrence's engraved works.

Oswald KNAPP — *An Artist's Love Story* 1904

George Somes LAYARD — *Sir Thomas Lawrence's Letter Bag* 1906

Sir Walter ARMSTRONG — *Lawrence* 1913. Contains a catalogue of Lawrence's works.

Douglas GOLDRING — *Regency Portrait Painter* 1951

Kenneth GARLICK — *Sir Thomas Lawrence* 1954
Contains a bibliography and a catalogue of Lawrence's works.

Kenneth GARLICK — *Walpole Society Vol. XXXIX* 1964
A catalogue of Lawrence's paintings, pastels and drawings which completely supercedes the previous catalogues.

Sir Oliver MILLAR — *The Later Georgian Pictures in the Collection of H.M. the Queen* 1969

ROYAL COMMISSION FOR HISTORICAL MANUSCRIPTS — *Catalogue of the Lawrence Correspondence in the Royal Academy Library* 1974

Kenneth GARLICK — *Sir Thomas Lawrence*
A complete catalogue of of oil paintings 1989

Kenneth GARLICK — *Sir Thomas Lawrence Portraits of an Age, 1790-1830,* 1993

Michael LEVEY — *Thomas Lawrence*, 2005

There are a number of articles on Lawrence and many references to him in periodicals, especially *The Burlington Magazine*, *Apollo* and *The Connoisseur*. These may be found in the artist indexes to the magazines. The third 'Burlington Lecture' was given in 1975 by Michael Levy on Lawrence's portrait of Pius VII; it was published in *The Burlington Magazine* in April 1975.

Much the most important collection of primary source material is the nine volumes of Lawrence papers in the Royal Academy Library. There are other important collections in the British Library, the library of the Victoria and Albert Museum, the Fitzwilliam Museum, Cambridge and the Beinecke Library, Yale University. Lawrence was a prolific letter writer and letters to and from him are to be found in many libraries and print rooms.